CADDY-TALK:
Psychology of Being a Great Golf Caddy

Vicki Aitken
BA, PGDipPE, MPhEd

Daniel A. Weigand
BSc, MSc, PhD

DAWVIJA PUBLISHING
Milton Keynes, U.K.

Published by DAWVIJA Publishing in 2007
92 Gaddesden Crescent, Milton Keynes, MK7 7SQ, U.K..

Printed by Jarvis and Co, Essex, U.K.

ISBN: 978-0-955-58590-6

ACKNOWLEDGMENTS

Vicki and Dan would like to thank in particular all the caddies, Steve, Mikey, Fooch, Fred, and the anonymous caddy (who knows who he is), for sharing their time, experience, and expertise with us for this book. A big thanks goes to Malcolm Evans, for his guidance, artistic insight, awesome cartoons, and patience with us. Thanks also to everyone who gave us their opinions and wisdom on the draft version(s) of this book: Judy Weigand, Michael Weigand, Liz McKinnon, Anne Laing (from Caddie Connect; thanks also for your invaluable ideas at the beginning of the project), Steve Walsh, Robin Bertaut, and Rod Gutry. Thanks Del, Nick, Claire and Broxy for your musical inspirations, Alison and Benn for your JPG expertise. Furthermore, we want to thank Tina Bonfield for advice on publishing and Rob Jarvis and his Dad Bob for an excellent printing job. Finally, we want to thank Tania Stiles (www.maia-internet.co.uk) for the brains behind the website.

Dan: Thank you Vicki, for your insight, experience, laughter, hard work, and patience; and of course, thanks to Judy, for her continued love and support in all that I do.

Vicki: Thanks Dan for your grammatical knowledge, time, patience, and dedication to the project—our skills matched beautifully! Thanks also to the Big G for kicking my motivation into gear when it wandered. And finally, thanks to my family, flat mates (past and present) and close friends for your love and support on many levels throughout the project.

ABOUT THE AUTHORS

Vicki Aitken, a New Zealander based in the U.K., is an experienced sport psychology consultant specialised in the game of golf (see www.vickiaitken.com). She is the "sport psychologist with the Ladies European Tour," where she has worked with players and caddies for over 7 years, helping them reach their personal bests and collecting 7 professional wins between them. Fully accredited with the British Association of Sport and Exercise Sciences, she has also worked with golfers of all levels and ages, as well as athletes in a variety of other sports including tennis and snowboarding throughout the U.K., Europe, and N.Z..

Dan Weigand, an American, is president of Achieve Acumen, Inc. (see www.AchieveAcumen.com). He is an internationally published researcher, specialising in motivation and performance enhancement, and an Association for Applied Sport Psychology certified consultant and fellow in sport psychology. He has worked with children, adolescents and adults, including amateurs, professionals and Olympians, from approximately 20 individual and team sports, in the U.S.A. and U.K.

CONTENTS

Chapter 1: INTRODUCTION

Why Read this Book?

Caddy-talk is the first book to outline a critical role in golf: the psychological aspects of being a great caddy. Being a great caddy is much more than carrying a bag: Great caddies are on-course sport psychologists. They also are there to help with all aspects of on- and off-course management. That's the purpose of this book: to teach these skills to caddies. Even if you think you have these skills, you probably can improve them.

Caddy-talk is the ultimate handbook on the psychology of caddying, answering your questions, regardless of whether you're a club-level or professional caddy!

It's a "how to" book, applying tried and tested performance-enhancing sport psychology techniques to the science of caddying. No other book offers this much information. Sure, there are books that provide insights of certain caddies or talk about the caddying experience, but none are instructional like this one.

The best feature of this book is that it's developed through interviews with some of the best caddies currently available. Quotes from in-depth interviews with Steve Williams (currently Tiger Wood's caddy), Mark Fulcher (currently caddying on the men's European Tour), Fred "Bassett" (24 years experience on the Ladies European Tour; LET), Mike Patterson (currently Karrie Webb's caddy), and an anonymous (and very well respected) tour caddy who works on the U.S. Ladies Professional Golf Association Tour and the LET, are woven into every chapter. Their insights provide excellent examples which highlight lessons learned from the authors' years of extensive research and consulting experience.

This book is also for every golfer!

Every chapter will highlight how the information discussed is important for players of golf, too. You will learn what caddies do to help their golfers play better, which you'll then be able to use in your own game. Players who regularly use caddies will learn what to look for when choosing a caddy; they'll also learn how to best work with a caddy to get the most out of their own game.

How the Book Came to be

The first author, Vicki Aitken, has worked as a sport psychology consultant for over six years on the LET. In those years, she's worked with a variety of golfers and caddies from various tours. Whilst working with these individuals, she came to realise that the role of the caddy, as the on-course sport psychologist, was not well covered in either academic or mainstream literature. She discussed this with the second author, Dan Weigand, an academic and consultant in sport psychology, and it was agreed to study this idea further. It was decided that it was necessary to talk with elite caddies about their experiences and see how those experiences meshed with the current literature. Vicki conducted the interviews with our expert caddies and then Vicki and Dan both used appropriate quotes to insert in to the chapters to help illustrate the points being made.

All of the interviews were approved by the caddies. Moreover, they have approved of the entire book. Therefore, we're satisfied that we've presented their ideas to the best of our abilities.

Organisation of the Book

The book is organised into five additional chapters and two appendices. Chapter 2 defines *caddy-talk*. It introduces the concept and describes the purposes of communication. It also discusses the process necessary for good communication. This chapter provides useful suggestions for sending and receiving effective messages. The focus is on turning the self-talk of caddies (what they think) into actual helpful recommendations that their players

2

will use. Lots of ideas are included! This chapter also introduces topics that are addressed in greater depth in the following chapters.

The purpose of Chapter 3 is to help you understand how to make good decisions. To do so, you'll need to know how to create a good game plan and set good goals. The pre-shot routine is also discussed because it is a necessary part of implementing a good game plan. Good decision making also depends upon a partnership based on confidence in each others' abilities; in other words, both caddy and player need to be able to trust each other to make good choices. So, in this chapter you'll learn how to develop confidence in yourself and in your partner. Of course, related to this is having positive self-talk. Therefore, you'll also learn how to develop positive self-talk while reducing your negative self-talk.

Unfortunately, there are barriers to effective caddy-talk. We discuss several of these in Chapter 4, including blaming the caddy for the player's mistakes, trust issues, caddies with dual roles (e.g., caddy and spouse/parent), and personality clashes. We'll provide suggestions for dealing with all of these potential problems.

Chapter 5 is about "switching off." What we cover in this chapter is the ability to not think about golf in playing downtime. No one can, or should, concentrate on their goals and strategy the entire time they're on the golf course. There has to be "down" time when you think about other things. In this chapter you'll learn when it's appropriate to think about your shots, and when it's okay not to think about them – to switch off. Great caddies know how to help their players switch on and off. We'll show you how to do this, including making suggestions for how conversation, games, music, and nutrition can help. This chapter will also include some reminders about fitness and equipment management.

We'll conclude the book in Chapter 6. We'll summarise what we've taught you and make suggestions for what to do next.

Finally, in the first appendix you'll see each caddy's case study. You will be able to read each caddy's story and opinions on various aspects of caddying and playing. We've also included some exercises for you in the second appendix; they're intended to help you become the caddy or player you want to be. The exercises will be discussed in detail where relevant.

Chapter 2: CADDY-TALK
It's not only what you say, but how you say it!

Caddy-talk refers to the communication process between golfers and their caddies that influences the performance, satisfaction, and enjoyment of both parties. It involves the caddy's self-talk, the golfer's self-talk, and the communication between them. The main purposes of effective caddy-talk are to build and/or maintain the golfer's confidence, focus attention to appropriate cues, help regulate arousal (excitement and/or anxiety), and facilitate the use of a pre-shot routine.

The golfer is the team's leader, the caddy is the information resource and the on-course mental skills coach; ultimately, decisions are made by the player, but the caddy's input is essential for good performance. The purpose of this chapter is to describe the purposes and processes of communication and suggest ways to improve effective communication. This chapter also introduces many of the topics covered throughout the rest of the book.

Purposes of Communication

Caddy-talk, a caddy's thoughts or what is said out loud, is intended to evaluate, inform, persuade, motivate, and problem solve. In other words, effective caddy-talk helps golfers to evaluate the situation (based on information gathered by the caddy) and decide on a course of action that the player feels confident in pursuing. Therefore, caddy-talk may include discussions about the golf course, the golfer's ability to perform a shot (including club selection), the golfer's experience in similar situations (ideally remembering/imagining success in similar situations), and considering problems (and solutions) associated with the situation. The caddy's responsibility is to provide enough information to be persuasive, while at the same time appreciating the fact that it is the player who must decide what to do (once all the information has been assessed). [See Chapter 3 for more on decision making.]

5

For example, if a caddy thinks his golfer should use a 7 iron, because the golfer successfully used a 7 iron in a similar situation, but the golfer wants to use an 8 iron because she's sure she can reach the green, although she's hitting into the wind, it's up to the caddy to try and persuade her that she wasn't able to reach the green with a 8 iron the last time she had this shot, without having to force the shot. Ultimately, if he can't easily convince the player to use the 7 iron, then he has to be willing to support the choice of the 8 iron (with great confidence) and see what happens. Of course, being persuasive requires being convincing, which requires sending effective messages.

> I'd say to her, even if I disagree with a club, and I have done...I'd always agree with her in the end. I would say 'that's a good club, I agree with you'....I'll say my opinion, and if she doesn't take my opinion, then what the hell, there's no point taking sides. – Mark Fulcher

The Process of Communication

The first thing to consider when thinking about communication is that it is a four-step process: (a) the sender thinks about the message (i.e., self-talk occurs), (b) the sender sends the message (e.g., verbally, in written form, or through non-verbal behaviour), (c) the receiver gets the message, and (d) the receiver responds to the message (i.e., self-talk occurs and a reply is sometimes sent or an action is made). Unfortunately, because most of us are not "mind readers," there's a potential for a breakdown in communication at each stage.

Let's look at each of these potential problems individually. First, the sender may not clearly understand what he wants to communicate (e.g., he isn't sure what to say or how to say it). This means that the message that's sent may be unclear. This could happen when one's self-talk isn't effective. This inner dialogue we have with ourselves can breakdown due to insufficient time to think things through completely. Before you want to communicate something to someone else, be sure you've talked to yourself about what you want to say. Make sure you know *exactly* what you want to say (and how you're going to say it).

Alternatively, the message may be clear but the method of communication isn't effective (e.g., it's too "noisy" and the message gets distorted when sent). For example, when out on the golf course, when another player is hitting her shot you may have to whisper to your player. If this happens, be sure to stand close to your player so she can hear you when talking to her. Another example might be when you're trying to debrief after a round. [See a detailed discussion of this later in this chapter.] You might be doing this over dinner, or in a crowded room, and it may be loud, and your player maybe uncomfortable or distracted by such an environment. Again, be sure you're able to talk effectively;

if not, wait until you're in a quieter more private place before discussing the day's play.

Of course, the message might be clearly considered and then sent correctly, yet still not heard. This could happen when the receiver isn't ready to hear the message (maybe she is thinking about something else and isn't paying attention to the message). For instance, if your golfer is thinking too much during a round, she may block out what you say, preferring to over-think something (usually something bad that has just happened) longer than she should. In this case caddies need to be able to sense that the golfer isn't thinking about the next shot and make her focus on what needs to be done—not what has happened (you should think about mistakes while debriefing, not while playing).

> You can sometimes see a player standing over a shot and you can detect they're not feeling comfortable….There is nothing wrong with saying 'hey get off it, y'know, re-think what you're trying to do,' that sort of thing. – Steve Williams

Finally, the message may be clearly considered, clearly sent, heard correctly, and the response isn't effective. This might happen when the receiver doesn't want to listen to the message. For example, a caddy gives "good'" advice to a golfer but the golfer has already made up his mind and therefore ignores the message (like choosing to use an 8 iron instead of a 7 iron). In this case, the message was sent correctly, but not effectively. Therefore, giving good advice means caddies have to send messages effectively— messages need to be persuasive if caddies are going to be helpful.

> I think the best caddies can read their player's minds…can see what they're thinking….You've gotta be able to put yourself in that person's shoes…to be able to see and…to think and…to look at the situation like you're in their shoes: 'What have they looked at?'

'How're they feeling?' 'What do they see?' – Steve Williams

Sending Effective Messages

Because there are times when the message isn't delivered effectively, there's a need to think about ways of sending better messages. This includes verbal and non-verbal messages, as well as messages conveyed in other ways (e.g., written). This section will focus on verbal and non-verbal communication, but many of these suggestions apply to other forms of communication as well (e.g., e-mails, faxes, letters, texts).

The first recommendation for effective verbal communication is to **be direct**: don't hint around the message or get someone else to communicate your message for you. Obviously, if it's just the caddy and player on the course together, there's no one else to help communicate messages, but when they're off-course (e.g., on the practice range, in the clubhouse, or even at home with the family), there may be times when caddies ask others to convey a message to their golfers. Try to avoid this. Having someone else convey a message for you allows opportunities for mistakes (e.g., saying the wrong thing, saying the right thing but with the wrong emotions). If the message is important, deliver it yourself. Even if you have to text or sms your player this is a safer and more direct form of communication than passing on a message via a third party.

Furthermore, caddies need to **be firm** in their recommendations to golfers. For example, if a caddy has effectively evaluated a golfer's upcoming shot, determined a potential strategy for executing the shot, and firmly believes in the recommendation, then she should speak with conviction. Again, as indicated above, the final decision is the golfer's, but players can attempt to change a caddy's mind about a strategy. If the caddy isn't convincing, the golfer may not accept the recommendation, and may play the wrong shot. Therefore, it's important to be direct. Say what you mean; mean what you say.

9

Always convey your thoughts on club choice directly. There needs to be no mince words as this may lead to confusion. – Anonymous Caddy

This means having enough relevant information to be persuasive. Caddies need to take lots of notes in their yardage books on what works and doesn't work so they'll be able to refer to their notes when suggesting a shot, club, strategy, etc. [See more on the use of a yardage book in Chapter 3.] If they can "prove" to their golfer that what they're suggesting is based on facts (previous performance) and the player's tendencies, then they'll be more convincing. In our example of the 7 instead of the 8 iron, if the caddy can show previously successful shots in a similar situation were made using the 7 iron, he'll be better at convincing his golfer that it's the right choice.

You tell her 'I think it's a seven iron' because of whatever reasons…'it's uphill,' 'it's downhill,' or…'y'know, the wind's here; that's why it's a seven iron, it's not an eight iron'….You gotta have a reason…like if it's either or, you gotta say…why…you can't really just say 'seven iron.' – Anonymous Caddy

In a related way, it's important to **own your messages**: use "I believe…" not "Most people think…" when trying to be persuasive. This may not seem relevant when discussing what caddies should or shouldn't do, but it is. For instance, a caddy might say, "Most of the caddies are recommending using a driver off the tee on this par 5, because the fairway is so wide, so you should too." An alternate, and better message would be, "Because you're hitting your driver so well today, and using it on this par 5 will allow you to go for the green in two, I'd recommend using the driver." Of course, if this golfer isn't hitting her driver well that day, maybe going for the green in two isn't a good idea. The message then might be, "This hole is a great birdie opportunity for you. Use your 3 wood off the tee, lay up on your second shot, and get it close with your third shot." In this scenario the driver isn't even mentioned! This scenario also reveals how important the caddy's self-talk is. The caddy has to think about what to say before saying it, taking into consideration the player's mind-set at the time; saying the wrong thing at the wrong time, could be disastrous.

> It's matter of fact; I give her facts and figures that's all....I make statements....For example, I give her the yardage...I tell her the wind direction and how far the pins on the green are and just give her the information she needs to know....Then she might ask me, 'what did we have yesterday?'...so I give her yesterday's yardage, coz I write it all down everyday...and we compare the two. Obviously, I don't say a club unless she asks me; if she asks me what club, then I'll tell her. I say what I think...I just dish the facts and the figures and then she'll ask and I'll tell her what I think.
> – Fred "Bassett"

Caddies must also **be complete and specific**: provide all the information necessary to fully understand your message (avoid assumptions). Give your player as much information as is necessary to be convincing. If this means referring to several pages of notes, do so. If this means forcing him to remember previous experiences, do so. If this means reminding him about today's strategy, do so. Golfers are notorious for letting their minds wander when they're supposed to be thinking about their next shot (it's okay to let them wander between shots; it's impossible to be totally focused all the time; see more on this topic in Chapter 5). Caddies must bring them back to earth, keeping them focused on the shot at hand. To do this, caddies must be able to rely on relevant, specific, and detailed reminders of what works.

> You might come across a particular shot where you know the player is not comfortable....You know you remind them, 'hey you've hit this shot a hundred times, a thousand times on the practice range; you

know how to do it, this is no different a situation. Block out the situation and make that same swing that you do on the practice range and go ahead.' – Steve Williams

Another important thing to remember is to **be clear and consistent**: avoid double messages. A common communication problem arises when you accidentally send two messages simultaneously. For example, a caddy might say to a golfer, "Normally, you should be assertive/aggressive (aggressive is the more common term in golf) on this hole and use your driver, but I think you should be conservative and use a 3 wood."

This message conveys two meanings: (a) normally you *are* and *should* be aggressive on this hole, and (b) there's some reason why you shouldn't be aggressive today. Obviously, this message isn't going to instil confidence in the golfer. [See more on the topic of confidence in Chapter 3]. The golfer isn't sure what to do. If she is more confident than the caddy, she wants to be aggressive, but also wants to pay attention to the caddy's suggestions. This could create indecision and perhaps anxiety, which will lead to muscle tension and poor execution of the shot.

An alternative and better strategy would be to clearly communicate concerns about being aggressive while also building confidence. For instance, the caddy might say, "Keeping the ball on the fairway is good on this hole and if you use a 3 wood you'll put yourself in a great place for your second shot." Nothing is said about what's "normal," there is less pressure, and no mixed messages are sent. The reminder about hitting the fairway, something all golfers want to do, clearly reminds the golfer to be conservative. What's normal is what's required for that shot, on that day, in those conditions to be optimally successful.

Don't mention the trouble! Any trouble on the course, you point that out during your practice rounds...out of bounds left, water on the right. You don't stand up on the tee box during a tournament and say negatives, you've done that in the practice rounds…so you don't; no negatives on the golf course, always positives…and little words to lift 'em or just little words of encouragement. – Fred "Bassett"

Stating your feelings clearly (i.e., not being afraid to show your emotions) is another recommendation for effective communication. Athletes, especially males, are often poor at being emotional. Yet, emotions influence our thinking. How we feel (e.g., happy, sad, angry, excited) can affect our thoughts so much that our attitudes and beliefs change. For example, when you're excited and confident about hitting a shot, you're more likely to be aggressive: you "go for it."

However, when you're angry and not so confident, you're unlikely to be aggressive; or, you still go for it but don't use your pre-shot routine and you hit a bad shot. [Read more about pre-shot routines in Chapter 3.] Either way, it's easy for your emotions to dictate your thinking. It's important for golfers to be open and honest about what they're feeling, not just what they're thinking because this allows a clear awareness of the situation. If the feelings aren't right, do something to change them. Don't take a shot until the emotions and thoughts are optimal for a confident, yet controlled shot.

For caddies, it's especially important to be aware of their player's emotions and be ready to help regulate them. In other words, a good caddy is able to "psych up" or help calm down his golfer. Arousal management is the responsibility of the caddy and the golfer, but on the course, it's the caddy's job to know what his player needs on any given shot.

When you can see them sort of coming off the rails a little bit and…maybe getting a little down hearted….I just try and gee them up a little bit. – Fred "Bassett"

Caddies should be ready to reach into their "toolbox" of ideas for increasing/decreasing arousal. They should have practiced with their players techniques that are sure to work. These could include emotionally-charged cues or key-words (e.g., "Let's do it!" "Come on!"), used to psych up or relaxing thoughts (e.g., "Relax, you can do it." "Take it easy."), along with some deep-breathing exercises to calm her down.

If she was in contention on Sunday, and she seemed like she was getting a bit tense, I'd sorta try to cool her down a little bit by saying 'hey...did you watch the cricket last night?' Y'know, obviously you try get her mind...off...thinking about the tournament...just try and relax her. – Anonymous Caddy

I think you need to know your player's personality....I've caddied for players who need...a certain pick up or who needs to be calmed down and I mean...certain players just need to be...let loose and if they're having a tantrum or whatever...it's sometimes best just to let them get it off their chest. – Mike Patterson

However, caddies need to be emotionally stable during competition: They need to be like a "rock," regardless of the situation. When not competing, caddies need to get to know their players and learn what their players want from them, in terms of emotions.

> I think you always have to be pretty much on a level emotionally...not get really high or really, really low. I mean a player doesn't need to see...their caddy jumping around....Just have the same aura about yourself...whether it's...on a Thursday morning or whether it's the Sunday afternoon...whether your player's made a double or made an eagle....Your player doesn't want to see you...down and depressed; they don't need to see that coming from their caddy....A player who's trying to win a tournament doesn't need to be calming their caddy down! I think that's pretty good for a caddy who can stay just level. – Mike Patterson

Some players want their caddies to be their friends; others, however, want their caddies to be just their colleagues (friendship isn't really wanted). Once you learn what your player wants from you, you'll be better able to express appropriate emotions.

> You need to be able to relate to different players. Women are different to men, they want friendship and loyalty. Men just want you to do the work and leave....LET players involve you in their life more than the men. – Mark Fulcher (paraphrased)

It is also very important to **focus on one thing at a time**: don't abruptly switch topics or talk about a situation that is in the past or more than one shot ahead. For instance, it is easy to get so involved in assessing the situation and planning for future shots that you don't focus on the shot at hand. Problems in communication often happen when caddies are trying to tell their golfers about what to do with their short irons while still on the tee (or talking strategy while getting ready to hit an approach shot). It's better to talk about what sort of tee shot is needed to get to the right spot on the fairway; then, once on the fairway, talk about the iron shot that will land where you want it on the green; then, once on the green, think about the putt.

Obviously, caddies need to be thinking ahead, planning tee shots which will create the ideal second shot, but the key to good communication is to know when to tell the golfer the plan. [See more about having a good game plan in Chapter 3.] Giving advice before it's needed may cause confusion (e.g., the golfer forgets about what to do on the tee because he or she is thinking about the iron shot). This means that caddies must organize their thoughts before speaking. Caddies need to know what to say, when to say it, and how to say it so that the message is clearly understood and effectively acted upon.

This next suggestion is a tricky one. Effective communication depends on **avoiding confrontations**. That is, avoiding arguments. It's important to deliver messages immediately: holding back may cause your feelings to intensify to the boiling point. We have a tendency to let anger "stew." We get angry, don't discuss the source of the anger, or try to resolve the problem; we then get even angrier and let the anger "erupt" into an argument. It's better to not let the anger stew. It's better to talk about the problem before it leads to an argument.

This type of problem can easily happen when there's a difference of opinion on a shot selection. The caddy suggests a club, the golfer doesn't want to use it, but doesn't explain why she doesn't want to use it; she uses it anyway, makes a poor shot, and blames (in her self-talk) the caddy. This may happen several times throughout a round until the golfer "blows up" and tells off the caddy; an argument ensues.

Avoiding arguments is about effective communication. Taking notice of all of the suggestions in this chapter will lead to effective communication and limit the occurrence of arguments. Ultimately, however, it's important to remember that the player has the final say in what happens. Caddies give advice; players make the shots. Keeping this in mind should prevent a lot of confrontations. Both individuals must be willing to work on developing good communication skills so that both are able to make/reject suggestions without an argument. The best way to do this is to be sure that you know why you want to make a suggestion (be sure you're ready with all the facts).

> I think when you are a caddy, you've got to work to think of the right thing to say at the right time and that's...fairly important: to be able to know when to say something and when not to say something....It's just something you learn with each player: when to speak to and when not to speak to them; and...it's something you've got to learn. It's something you've got to realise when you form a relationship with a player, when he likes to be spoken to, or doesn't like to be spoken to and when he needs something positive said....If you want to have a relationship, that's one of those things you work out with a player, coz when the time comes you know when to say something: what he likes to hear and then what he doesn't like to hear. – Steve Williams

Another strategy for avoiding confrontation is to **be supportive**: don't deliver messages filled with sarcasm, threats, judgments, or negative comparisons. This seems like such an obvious statement that it's not worth mentioning, but unfortunately these things happen, especially with multiple role caddies such as spouses, partners or parents.

Sarcasm, or unintentional mockery, often said as a joke, isn't helpful. A caddy might say to a golfer, "You can't get to the green from here, that would take a miracle; who do you think you are, Tiger Woods?!" This message isn't funny (unless, of course, you're working with Tiger Woods!); moreover, it makes a negative judgment about the golfer's ability, especially in comparison to Tiger Woods, arguably the greatest golfer of all time. The intent might be to lessen the pressure on the golfer. The caddy might be thinking that joking around will ease the pressure and reduce the potential for anxiety. In fact, the opposite is likely. The golfer's confidence might be weakened when he realizes he isn't Tiger Woods. Try avoiding this type of joking around and instead focus on what the golfer can do. For instance, taking a penalty drop rather than hitting the ball might be a better strategy for optimal scoring.

Try and avoid these sarcastic, negative, and judgmental responses:

Golfer: "Think I'm going to drown myself in the lake."
Caddy: "Think you can keep your head down that long?"

Golfer: "I'd move heaven and earth to break a hundred on this course."
Caddy: "Try heaven, you've already moved most of the earth."

Golfer: "Do you think my game is improving?"
Caddy: "Yes sir, you miss the ball much closer now."

Golfer: "Do you think I can get there with a 5 iron?"
Caddy: "Eventually."

Golfer: "You've got to be the worst caddy in the world."
Caddy: "I don't think so, sir. That would be too much of a coincidence."

Golfer: "Please stop checking your watch all the time. It's too much of a distraction."
Caddy: "It's not a watch—it's a compass."

Golfer: "How do you like my game?"
Caddy: "Very good sir, but personally, I prefer golf."

Golfer: "Do you think it is a sin to play on Sunday?"
Caddy: "The way you play, sir, it's a sin on any day."

Golfer: "This is the worst course I've ever played on."
Caddy: "This isn't the golf course. We left that an hour ago."

Golfer: "That can't be my ball, it's too old."
Caddy: "It's been a long time since we teed off, sir."
(Author unknown)

Reinforce with repetition (i.e., repeating key points of your message) is another strategy for effective communication. As indicated above, breakdowns in communication can occur when the message is received. The golfer might not hear or understand the message the first time it's sent. So, send it again, and again, if necessary. Try rephrasing the message by using different words. This may be especially important if your player's first language is different than yours.

When you talk with them, players are very predictable; surely y'know when you get into a situation, or something, it's obvious you don't want to say the same things every time because...it's a bit like a broken record....You always like to say something different, but kind of get it across the same way. But not always say the same thing, so your player actually hears the message...you're trying to convey the same message, but you're always getting it across in different ways. – Steve Williams

Related to this is the need to be sure your message was accurately received. This means watching for verbal (and non-verbal) cues. These signals can include statements (e.g., "OK, I understand") or actions (e.g., a head nod of approval). You can also reinforce by using consistent non-verbal communication. Non-verbal communication includes how you say something (e.g., the tone of your voice), your facial expressions, and your body language (i.e., posture).
Non-verbal messages often convey your intentions better than verbal messages. For example, a caddy that is

19

trying to build confidence in a golfer, and says "Go for it" but in a whisper, more than an excited shout, isn't conveying confidence. There's a mixed message being sent. Furthermore, it's the non-verbal message that's likely to be received (people tend to believe non-verbal messages more than verbal messages). In addition, non-verbal messages are usually not under conscious control so they're harder to hide. Therefore, it's very important to be aware of your non-verbal messages: Be sure they're consistent (i.e., they match) with your verbal messages.

The last recommendation about sending effective messages is to make your message appropriate for the receiver: **know your audience**. Obviously, in this case, know your player.

Knowing your player; knowing when to say something; and you never get it right all the time...there's no quick way of doing it, but conversation helps obviously....If you're just going to walk round and trudge along ten yards behind with the bag, you're not going to learn much....You're not going to learn their personality or anything. You've got to be upside them and talk...but if they don't want that, then you'll soon know; they'll soon let you know without being rude....All girls are different; all people are different...you get different kinds of personalities...so...you know the ones that are fiery...you're a little bit wary of them....Watch people even if you're not with them, even if you're not working for them. If you're paired with them, you can watch, you can see people's reactions. Sometimes...you can see their personalities. – Fred "Bassett"

Everyone is different, so it's important to know how to communicate differently depending on the person you're talking to. This also means that some caddies are better suited to work with certain golfers: their personalities match. [See Chapter 4 for more information about personalities.] If communication problems happen, first try the strategies suggested above (and in Chapter 4). If they don't work, maybe the fit between caddy and golfer isn't a good one. It might be a good idea to change partnerships. It's very important that communication is optimally effective: it benefits both parties; but, if nothing can be done to make the partnership work, maybe it's time to break it up.

I was with Ali Nicholas four years, was with Laura Davies quite a while. I think...a long-term caddy-player relationship is good but...sometimes I think you need to freshen it up; it can get dull, coz...it could end up stale, but I think it's good to work together long-term. You can get two who really fit well; with a bit of security there, you can work much better....I think it would be fantastic if you find the right gel. For a player, it needs to be right. And there are so many different varieties of characters out there; there're so many different caddies. – Mark Fulcher

Debrief Sessions

An essential aspect of getting to know your player is the debrief session. You should take time after every round (and probably after each practice session) to discuss what went right today and what went wrong.

You'll want to focus first on what went well—what worked. Remember each hole, if possible. Think about the advice you gave your golfer. Did you have a good game plan? Was it effectively communicated? Were you persuasive? Was the advice good? Did your player hit the shot she wanted? If not, why not? After thinking about your successes, think about what you could have done better today. Think about each hole again. What went wrong? Was there something we could have done differently? Once you've identified what worked and didn't work, you're now ready to think about how to improve on your success and reduce the failures.

This is also an excellent time to get to know what your golfer wants from you if you are new to the relationship or if you have been working together for a while it can help you avoid getting complacent. You can talk about things on the practice area, or maybe in the locker room, or perhaps over a meal. You might want to write things down in a journal, to remind yourself what he likes and doesn't like, or what you need to do to better prepare yourself for the next day. The benefit of a debrief session is that it's done off the course, when you're both calm and thinking clearly. If done correctly, your communication process should be at its best and you'll really get to know each other.

> Usually…if I'm working with somebody, I ask them 'do you like to talk between shots?' Some don't….I ask them if they want small talk. Basically I'm just relaxed between shots…being myself…but some people don't, they prefer to be blinkered….I usually…tell them, if it's like the first tournament, if there's…anything that you want to say at the end of the week, say it…because…no offence is taken. I

have to learn…what you want, coz if you don't tell me I won't know….I don't take it as criticism….I'd rather be told. And there's nothing worse than, if I'm doing something wrong, or the wrong way, and they don't like it and there's friction….I want to know. Yeah, I do approach them about it on the practice ground or off the course mainly, not on the course…off the course, when we'd finished. Talk can correct it…or try to correct it…but if I can't correct it we part company….I like to stay friends. – Fred "Bassett"

After a round…you actually…sorta summarise how the day went, where you did particularly well, good area, or you had trouble with this hole, whether we can work it out…when you go to practice tee afterwards. A lot of times you go to the practice tee and you've played well, you just go to the tee to wind down, some days you go to the practice tee to work on things. You might…tell the player…what you saw…that you perhaps think you saw earlier on that he was doing wrong today, how he was swinging it….Or just say 'we had a bit of trouble on this hole' or 'we struggled on this hole, perhaps we should play it this way tomorrow' or…things like that. – Steve Williams

Humans are creatures of habit and will tend to react the same way to certain situations time after time. In this way, as a caddy, it is possible to learn how your player likes to be talked to and about what kind of things.

It is possible to shortcut some of this learning process by speaking to your player about what she likes before and after rounds. This can be especially useful early on in the caddy-player relationship when you are establishing your patterns of interactional behaviour. Ask your player what she liked and disliked about how you dealt with certain situations. Was there something that she liked in particular that you ought to do again? Or was there something that you need to do differently or better next time? Unless you ask, your player may not tell you. If your player does not tell you then you do not have an opportunity to improve.

Conclusion

In conclusion, it's not only what you say, but how you say it that makes it effective communication. Caddies and golfers must be able to effectively communicate to perform at their best. This requires an open, honest sharing of ideas and emotions, especially off the course. It also requires an awareness of what works and doesn't work, depending on the caddy-player relationship. But most of all, it depends on the caddy being diligent, knowledgeable, and persuasive.

What this Means for the Caddy

For caddies, caddy-talk is about helping your player succeed. It's about knowing what to say and what not to say. It's about knowing when to try to make suggestions and when to shut up—it's about being persuasive, yet knowing when to back off and let the player decide what to do. It's about knowing your golfer's thoughts, emotions, and behaviours— and using that knowledge to help him develop a strategy for optimal performance. Caddies know that they're there to assess the situation and provide helpful advice. They also know that, in general, they know what's best for their golfers. But to effectively communicate, you also need to understand that you have to get to know your player well so you'll be able to make suggestions that are accepted without controversy.

What this Means for the Player

For golfers, caddy-talk is about letting your caddy help you succeed. They know (or should know) a lot about your strengths and weaknesses. They know your tendencies. They know when you should play conservatively or aggressively. They know what's working and not working. Listen to them! Have regular debriefing sessions with your caddy. Get feedback from him about what's working and isn't working. Let him help you develop strategies for your success. Listen to him when he is suggesting shots to hit. Caddies want to help, they want you to be successful – it makes them happy and satisfied which makes them want to work even harder for you.

Because caddy-talk requires a two-way communication process between caddy and golfer, it also means that golfers need to work on their own communication skills. You need to develop your own self-talk. When challenging your caddy's suggestions, ensure you are able to provide facts as this will help earn his respect. The better you are at effective communication, the more you'll benefit from your caddy-talk and the more successful you'll be.

Chapter 3: DECISION MAKING
Choosing which shot to play!

The purpose of this chapter is to consider the aspects of good decision making. In Chapter 2 we outlined what caddy-talk is and discussed how important good communication is for caddies to help golfers achieve their best success. Similarly, in this chapter we'll highlight some of the things that influence the communication process.

Good decisions are often based on having a good game plan, so we'll start there. This includes knowing how to best use a yardage book. Having a good game plan also requires having good goals, so we'll describe what kinds of goals you need to set. Then, we'll focus on the need to be confident, where you'll learn ways to develop confidence, including having a good competition routine (including a pre-shot routine). Related to this is the need for positive self-talk. We'll focus on how you can improve your positive self-talk while reducing your negative self-talk. Finally, we'll discuss how the final decision belongs to the golfer. Caddies can influence the decision, but ultimately it's the player's choice.

Game Plans

Creating a game plan is an important part of playing successful golf. This is also the crux of a caddy's job. Professional tour caddies are some of the best experts from whom everyone can learn how best to use their yardage book and set game plans.

Great caddies and players figure out how best to play each hole in advance: They take into consideration the ability of the player and how to play each hole to the player's strengths. For example, if there is a lay-up hole they will ensure that they have the yardage that suits a full wedge or a particular full club (in which they have the most confidence or ability) for maximal control. This gives the player the best chance to put the ball "stiff" next to the pin—or to even hole the ball! A good game plan will also help players avoid playing their weak shots. For example, if a player is not feeling confident on long bunker shots you should play the hole so that a missed shot puts you into the grassy mounds front left of the green, avoiding the bunker, setting up for an easier shot onto the green. Good caddies would encourage their players hitting their approach shot to aim for their "safe zone" the left side of the green in this instance.

Good game plans are ideally set together as a team— where both the player and caddy look at the pros and cons of playing certain holes in particular ways. Good game plans take into account changes of wind or weather or speed of greens. If you lay up on a par 5 into little or no head wind, perhaps with a down-hole wind you can easily go for the green in two.

> When you've got carries over bunkers or carries over water; if it's into the wind…you wouldn't go for it, you'd lay up…short of the trouble; but if it's downwind, based on the yardage, you change your game plan, coz you can get there in two….You just have to be flexible a bit, but you go out with a game plan….You have to have one…what's the point of all the practice rounds if you don't make any plans? That's why you have two practice rounds. – Fred "Bassett"

Thinking of all the alternatives that might possibly occur on each hole prior to teeing it up on the first day of competition allows the player and caddy to be fully prepared and confident for whatever might happen on the day.

Furthermore, being fully prepared also requires considering in advance when to play conservatively and when to play aggressively. For example, Steve Williams believes in having a variety of different game plans for certain situations that you can find yourself in on the last day of a tournament:

> I think one of the most important things…when you are a caddy, is to look at the last three or four holes of a tournament and how you're going to play those

holes (a) if you've just got a tie and your leading, (b) if you're two or more ahead, or (c) if you're behind.

This is particularly applicable to match play rounds, as the decision to play certain holes is similarly influenced by your opponents and their performance. However, most players in normal stroke play rounds will have fewer variables to influence them. The idea behind setting a game plan and knowing in what type of circumstances you will change your plan means, **with discipline**, you will be less likely to allow your emotional reactions to dictate your choice in game plan tactics. Making your game plan decisions in the rational light of day, away from the heat of competitive play, allows you to make the best possible course management decisions, therefore producing the best possible results.

In order for you to create a good game plan, you'll need to know how to best use a yardage book. The yardage book is the ultimate tool for recording all the notes and information you need for implementing your game plan.

Most caddies and/or players will check that the yardages in the book that they buy from a tour yardage book-maker or from a local pro-shop are correct. Most caddies use either a laser or pace the yardages (regardless of whether they operate in yards or metres). Some caddies will also laser holes with uphill or downhill slopes to assess the degree of slope. Caddies using this system for every plus (for uphill) or minus (for downhill) will add or subtract accordingly the number of yards to the overall total in which they compute the final yardage and from which they select their club. Checking yardages and slopes are done usually on a Monday of a tournament week or before they play a practice round.

Walking the course gives you an opportunity to see it from different angles (e.g., you can look at the holes from the green to tee, which can reveal architectural illusions) and allows you to focus on the best target areas to put the ball.

A lot of players and caddies that you watch...they'll calculate each shot as X amount uphill or X amount downhill or take off this amount for wind, or this sort of thing, but...it's feel. I'd rather just give the yardage and say it's this much or it's downwind…so it makes it more of a feel judgment then…I just give the pure yardage and say it's a little bit uphill or a little bit downwind….I caddy more by feel….I'm more of a feel person. – Steve Williams

Most caddies when first taking on new players will keep a list of their players' clubs and how far they hit each on the full, and if appropriate, the average run out.

When it comes to mathematics, both caddies and players need to check that they choose the right dot from which they take yardage. One way to do this is by highlighting each dot and matching the number in your yardage book with the same colour.

Some caddies always walk the yardage off the ball to the following dot so they can add it on straight away. Others are happy either adding or subtracting from the nearest dot to make sure they have the most accurate yardage. Some caddies like to circle the numbers in the landing area (as per the example above) to minimise the likelihood of choosing an incorrect number. But you need to ensure that when you are subtracting that the ball is after the dot and when adding that the ball is before the dot you are using. Create a system that works to your strengths and allows you to be consistent and accurate.

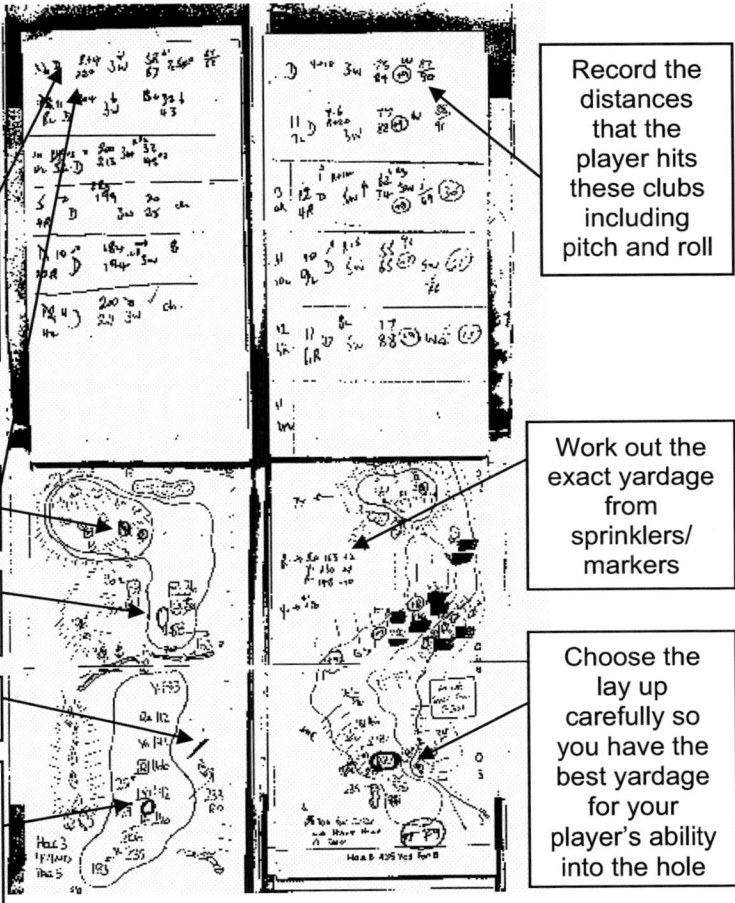

Record what clubs your player hits in practice and in each round played

Record the distances that the player hits these clubs including pitch and roll

Record the pin position

Work out the exact yardage from sprinklers/ markers

Mark in the lay up area

Target line

Choose the lay up carefully so you have the best yardage for your player's ability into the hole

Mark in the landing area/ finishing up

Examples from a professional caddy's yardage book

On the blank page above the diagram of the hole, caddies and or players will record a variety of information and statistics from each round. Players or caddies using a published book purchased from a pro-shop can either add in blank pages or scribble around the sides of the page. Most players/caddies using a standard tour book will divide the blank page into six spaces for four rounds of the tournament and two practices rounds. In each space they will record targets from tees, lines into holes, pin positions, yardage, all clubs hit, and the yardage the ball pitches onto the green and then releases. Some caddies also record statistics such as score, fairways hit in regulation, greens hit in regulation, up and downs, and putts, in order that they stay aware of their players' strengths and weaknesses and can encourage practice in the appropriate areas of the game.

Goals

In order for your game plan to be effective, you'll also need to set goals. All golfers need a clear focus of where they are going and what they are intending on achieving and even more importantly knowing how they are going to achieve this. Whilst the caddy does not need to know every last goal that the player has set, it can be a good idea to know about the goals that will impact upon their job together. Below we'll discuss goals that *don't* need to be shared with caddies (although they **can** be) and goals that *should* be shared with all caddies. We'll also mention a few goals specifically for caddies.

Goals That Don't Need to be Shared

Outcome goals focus on the ultimate result, such as wanting to win a tournament or beat an opponent in match play. The best thing about outcome goals is that they are highly motivating for a player, and if you are talking about golfers who are either playing professional or elite amateur golf, then it is strongly recommended that they set these types of goals.

Outcome goals will help a player get out of bed to practice in the morning and will help keep the spark of fire in her heart going when she faces a long hard season ahead of her. Unfortunately, outcome goals are not easy to achieve because golfers have limited control over them. If golfers wish to finish in the top 10 of a tournament (whether at club or tour level), they have no control over what everyone else in the field does that week. Your golfer may play the best golf of her life, but still finish outside the top 10, thus failing to achieve her goal!

Performance goals, on the other hand, focus on specific performance factors such as shooting a round of 70 or less, or having less than 36 putts in a round. You can also have performance goals for things like number of fairways hit during a round or greens reached in regulation.

Performance goals have a lot in common with outcome goals in that they can also be very motivating. Performance goals are goals that are set against yourself and your past performances (i.e., they're your personal bests). Every time a golfer goes out to play to his handicap or better he is setting himself a performance goal. A golfer's handicap is a measure of his average golfing ability which is marked by a number—like all performance goals.

Wanting to lower one's handicap or break par for the first time are very motivational goals that will get you out practising and working on your game more often; however, performance goals are also not totally within the golfer's control! Golfers may have between 60 to 90% of performance goals within their control. But if the ball decides to kick right out of bounds or left into the fairway, that is not in the player's control—an element of luck or unpredictability certainly exists within the realm of course layout and is compounded by weather fluctuations. For these reasons a player may do all the right things and still fail to reach a performance goal in a competition!

However, performance goals are great for players during their practice sessions. You can create all kinds of scenarios on the driving range, or during a practice round, where you try to improve your previous best performance. For example, you can see how many out of ten tries you can get the ball to draw just the way you want it to. In follow-up sessions, you'll try to improve on the number you hit correctly. Be creative! Think of lots of performance goals to work on when practicing—however, start slowly; have only a few performance goals initially. Once you get the hang of it

34

you can add more. We've included an exercise (Appendix B1) to help you with your goal setting.

Players do not necessarily need to share these motivational type goals with their caddies, because they merely help motivate them to perform to their best. However, by players sharing their outcome and performance goals with their caddies: (a) they will have someone else to help them be accountable, (b) caddies will be able to then directly and actively support their players and their pursuit of these goals, and (c) they can help ensure that the process goals—what they do on course—will go together with the motivational goals. The caddy can make sure that the process does not work to undermine the overall goals.

The player is like the captain of the team and the caddy is one of the crucial team members. What team captain (e.g., in football, basketball, rugby, hockey) would go into a game or match and not tell their team members what they were aiming to do and what the game plan is? In much the same way golfers would benefit from all their team members knowing what the overall outcome and performance goals are.

Goals That Should be Shared

Process goals are the "how to" goals of golf. They focus on developing your procedure. If you wish to win a competition or tournament you also need to plan these goals. Achieving process goals helps you achieve your outcome and performance goals! For example, a mentally strong player will know if she focuses on the target over the ball, does her pre-shot routine every time, and keeps her self-talk positive, it gives her the best chance to achieve her outcome and performance goals. These are processes.

Furthermore, process goals help you connect and get into a peak performance state, also called being in "flow," or being in "the zone." Getting into the zone is when everything seems to just work, you can't do anything wrong. Obviously, getting into the zone is what you're trying to achieve every time you lace up your shoes and head for the course.

Fortunately, good process goals are easy to achieve (a young child could do them) and they are 100% within the player's control. If you have total control over goals it means that you can achieve them **every** time that you play! But of course this requires discipline and this is where the caddy can help.

All golfers need to share these goals with their caddies as the caddy can then help them be accountable; but more importantly, can help them achieve these goals. If players start verbally abusing themselves caddies can encourage them and help them change their negative self-talk into positive self-talk (there's more on this topic later in this chapter). They can help them to focus on the target, by reminding them of what the target is on each hole. And they can call their player off the ball if they haven't done their routine properly. This way the process goals become a shared responsibility, although ultimately the buck stops with the player, the player can delegate some of the responsibility, but if it is or is not achieved, then it's the player who takes the credit or blame. The player, the team captain, has the greatest responsibility.

Whilst it is the player's responsibility to set and be accountable for achieving the goals, the caddy can actively encourage this process. The caddy can ask what the player's outcome and performance goals are, and especially the on-course process goals and game plan to achieve all of their goals. Caddies don't have to wait for their players to tell them their goals; they can take the initiative and ask. One caddy we know (who wished to be anonymous) establishes the communication early on in the relationship and when necessary will ask to speak to the player after a round to discuss goal strategies:

> You can only play one shot at a time, so…set the goal to shoot sixty-six; I mean you can do it but… I think it's bad actually…you can only take one shot at a time…so I think…a good goal's to…give a hundred percent to every shot; that'd be a better goal.

Goals for Caddies

All caddies, like their players, ought to set goals for themselves. In particular process goals—the goals that will help them do their job well and keep their mind on the job—are great for caddies to set. A good process goal for caddies might be to do their own routine well. One tour caddie we know had a goal to ensure that he walked out to the middle of the fairway and checked that he had the right yardage dot, especially when his player hit his ball into the rough or another fairway. These are little things that you can do as a caddy that are easy to achieve and are 100% within your control.

One final thought on goal setting. Good goal setting requires golfers gaining as much objective information about their strengths and weaknesses as is possible to discover. Obviously, you'll want to set goals to minimise your weaknesses and increase your strengths. Who better than your caddy to provide you with this information? Therefore, when you're identifying the things you need to work on, and you set goals to achieve them, you'll want to work with your caddy. Caddies need to be aware that they have a lot to say which should help their players improve. Helping them set goals can be a major benefit to their success.

Confidence

If you have a good game plan, and you set good goals, you will be more confident to achieve your goals. Of course, there are other ways to increase your confidence. One way is to have a consistent competition routine.

Competition Routines

The best way to get into the zone is to have a consistent strategy for success. Having a consistent routine before, during, and after competition is very important for creating consistent feelings of confidence.

During performance, players and caddies need to be carrying out their pre-shot routines. Players' pre-shot routines contain all the facets that they need to prepare both mentally and physically to play each shot to the best of their ability. For example, you think about your game plan, factor in the weather and hole lay-out, imagine where the ball is going to go, take a practice swing or two, take a deep breath and let it out, focus on the target, and then let it rip.

Successful golfers will do the same routine consistently; that is, they will go through the same actions and thoughts on every shot, and if timed, it will be precise down to the last second. Smart golfers will also regularly check their routines (like they would their grip and set up) to ensure that they are still doing what they think they are doing, and that each step still serves a purpose or function in helping them play their best possible shot.

Caddies who understand and are aware of their players' pre-shot routine will be in a better position to be able to help their players carry them out. Taking time to both observe and discuss this with their players off the course can help caddies' confidence in, for example, calling their player off the ball when they fail to execute the routine properly during a round. If players fail to carry out their pre-shot routines exactly, it usually means that they are distracted, unconfident, or uncertain. If any player fails to carry out her routine properly she will not play the shot well. If both caddy and player are aware of the player's routine, and work together to make sure it is carried out on every shot, this will help eliminate many of the player's bad shots.

Caddies ought to also have their own pre-shot routines where they go through a set procedure prior to giving information to their player. How far out from the ball do you cut conversation and pull your yardage book out? When do you start pacing the yardage, or start assessing wind and lie conditions? When is the best time to start discussing the club choice with your player, given his pre-shot routine?

> With the players I've worked for…you get into a routine of how you talk about a shot and…as I've said to you…I've always had my way of doing things but that's…had to change around players and how…they want things done…. Some players like to take more responsibility themselves and some players…might put more responsibility on the caddy. – Mike Patterson

Players, you can also expand your competition routine to include what you do the night before, or the morning before your round, or even after the round is over (e.g., a consistent debrief session). Obviously, caddies can help with all of this planning.

Pre-performance routines include what a player likes to do in preparation for a tournament and each round—it is a structured and organised plan of thoughts, feelings, and actions. What do you like to do in the days leading up to the tournament, the night before, and on the day of play prior to teeing it up? A good caddy and player team will figure out what works best for them leading up to a tournament. For example, most tour caddies like to walk the course on a Monday before their player arrives at the course. Some tour players like to take Monday's off and treat it as a travel and rest day. Tuesday's maybe a practice round and then range and short-game practice, where player and caddy have an opportunity to discuss their game plan and work on game weaknesses. Wednesday may be pro-am day or another opportunity to have a practice round to test-run the game plan. Thursday is play day, and depending on tee times, both caddy and player will have their own routines of what they like to do to prepare to perform at their best. Caddies, like their players, will have their own routines that they like to go through prior to playing each day. Serious caddies, whenever possible, will walk the course before playing.

> Go out on the course...and have a good look at the course....You see a lot of caddies...they just buy the yardage book these days and they've been here last year and they don't go out. They walk around the course in a practice round with a player. But go out there and make sure you scout the course properly. Prior to your round starting, and time permitting, ensure that you go out and look at HOW the course is playing, how the greens are, 'are the greens soft?' How the pin positions are today. At certain events...particularly the British Open...you are actually allowed to go out and... walk on the course; a lot of courses won't allow you to walk on them....Little things like that. Anything that you can do, that you think you might be able to get an edge with, you want to do. – Steve Williams.

Post-performance routines, much like pre-performance routines, are what players like to do after playing and in preparation for the next day's play. Find out what works best for you. Some players always like to hit balls after a round and others don't. If your player likes to hit balls it ought to have purpose. Does it serve to build confidence for the next day or does it potentially undo current confidence and or add to the frustration levels? Having an opportunity to debrief on what worked and what needs to be improved or altered for the next day [see Chapter 2 for more details on communication and the debriefing process] is a crucial part of a good post-performance routine. Good caddies will make notes and make adjustments to yardage books as a result of agreed game plan changes. Once the day is over it's important to forget about it, switch off and relax in the evening so you can be in the best physical and mental state to carry out your pre-performance routine and play the next day.

The purpose of letting the caddy help with these plans is that it lessens the load for the golfer, and that's a caddy's job. It also makes it easier for the player to get into the zone—with less to think about, the player can focus on building his own confidence level.

Self-talk

As we continue our discussion on developing confidence, we need to discuss self-talk some more. Remember, we introduce self-talk in Chapter 2—it is the first step in caddy-talk! Every caddy and player who is self-confident will have good self-talk. Positive self-talk is essential when you're trying to influence golfers. A confident caddy or player will think positively and realistically because his thoughts will be based on good goals, whereas an unconfident caddy will think negatively and unrealistically.

> Make...sure they have the right information and...never humming and arhing about what you're...suggesting that they do...and...just sounding confident...yourself about what...they have to do. – Mike Patterson

Positive self-talk is simply saying or thinking what you want to do; it's a reminder of what you're trying to achieve. For example, a player might say to himself "Let's hit the ball down the middle of the fairway" to help him focus on what he wants to do with the ball. Or another golfer might say "let's do it" to help psych herself up. A caddy, in contrast, might say to himself, "be confident when telling her which club to use." In all three cases you're saying to yourself what you want to accomplish—it's positive!

In contrast, negative self-talk is more complicated. There are three types of negative self-talk. The most obvious one is **self-abuse**. For instance, a caddy may think "You idiot, you totally stuffed up there, you'll probably get fired now!" Instead, you want to talk to yourself encouragingly like you'd expect your best friend to: "Come on forget that mistake, focus on what you are doing now and you can win her trust back!"

Another type of negative self-talk, **pressure statements**, are a little more subtle. For example, "You need to get the green read right this time." This creates a black and white situation for yourself, where if you don't succeed, the other option is clear failure, with consequences such as the worst case scenario of getting fired.

The third type of negative self-talk involves using the word **not**. Essentially, the brain fails to register negatives, including don't, can't, or won't.

Close your eyes now for a minute and try <u>not</u> to think of your favourite ice cream. Don't think of that ice cream for the next 10 seconds...

So what did you think of? Most people see the ice cream! This happens because it's essentially as if your brain works in pictures. Unfortunately, the brain doesn't have a picture for **not**, so you by default think of the ice cream. The only people who succeed at doing this task actively replace the ice cream picture thought with something else such as a drink. And this is exactly the process you need to go through in your own mind when you experience any of these negative thoughts. In other words, you can control your thoughts!

The best way to get rid of negative thoughts is to replace them with something positive instead. Trying to block them out or ignore them will not be as effective, as we are all products of society which teaches us to think negatively. You only need to spend time in a clubhouse as golfers come in from a round of golf: Most players will be more comfortable telling you about their bad shots than they will about their good ones. Or for another example, you need only listen to a parent trying to correct one of their children and they say: "don't do that!" and the parent wonders why minutes later the naughty child is still doing it.

Being able to change your own self-talk requires a degree of self-awareness. You first need to know what kinds of thoughts you have when caddying or playing. Are they negative or positive? If they are negative you need to choose to stop and change them to something positive. You do this by replacing them with positive statements (this is exactly what you do out loud when you detect your player saying something negative). We've included an exercise (Appendix B2) to help you identify your negative self-talk. You'll be able to identify when it occurs and figure out the kind of positive self-talk needed instead.

We are all human and may think negatively from time to time; the important thing is whether we are aware of it or not. If we know we are doing it, then we have the power to change it. When you do that you will help keep your confidence afloat.

Developing Confidence

Caddies and golfers need to be supremely confident in their own abilities. Self-confidence can be defined as believing in your own ability to do the best you can. Confident golfers and caddies expect to be successful and believe in their ability to perform successfully. Being confident doesn't mean you'll perform well, but you won't perform well without it!

Nervous caddies who act unsure, or who are focusing on not making a mistake, will fail to instil confidence in their players. Instead caddies need to have solid self-belief in their abilities or at least appear as if they do. You can always "Fake it, 'til you make it." When you think and act confidently your player is more likely to trust you and more likely to take your advice on board when it comes to choosing a shot and club to play.

> What I like…about working for…my current player is if we disagree about a club and I'm right and she's wrong, she will tell me…she'll say 'Oh sorry Fred'…she'll apologise to me…and…there's no conflict. The fact that we disagree doesn't create a conflict….Some players will hit the shot and they'll blame you for everything….They'll never admit that they've made a mistake but…she does…which is better. It creates a better working relationship, because if you're gonna get blamed for everything…it puts you on edge…and you can sort of drift…to the attitude where you might sit on the fence a little bit…instead of committing yourself to what you think…coz you don't want to commit yourself in case you get blamed for something that's not your fault….You must be one hundred percent positive in your own ability. You know you would be found out if you weren't. You don't want to be a 'yes' man. – Fred "Bassett"

I'm not sure about other caddies, but...sometimes I feel...a few butterflies; I wouldn't say it was nervousness, more just a few butterflies...before you tee off in the final group on a Sunday....I think that's perfectly natural....I think I hide it well, or that's what I've been told anyway. – Mike Patterson

Caddies, like players, can work on improving their self-confidence. There are many things you can do to increase your confidence. One way is to achieve your goals. Performance accomplishments build confidence (not only in your ability, but in your ability to set goals too!). Another thing you can do is to imagine success. Just like using imagery to help you see the roll of a putt, you can imagine yourself achieving your goals.

A really good exercise for proving to yourself why you should be confident is to sit down and see how quickly you can fill a sheet of lined paper with bullet points of why you are a great caddy/player (see Appendix B3). What qualities do you possess that make you a great caddy? Are you personable; good at doing yardages; cool, calm and collected under pressure; have a sense of humour; are passionate about golf; and/or a quick learner? If so, then you should be confident! If not, then you'll need to work on developing your confidence. Of course, you could learn from what expert caddies have to say about what it takes to be a confident caddy:

Get all the basics right....Be on time, clean the clubs, put up the yardage, walk the course, get as much information as you can....Just do all the basics and look after your player. – Mark Fulcher

I think punctuality is the main thing. You gotta be here...and then you don't want to turn up at the course without a wash and a shave in the morning....But I'm...old school...you get some of the younger lads who couldn't [care less]. I'm not saying that does make them any worse as a caddy, but it's just that I'm a bit of an old fart, I s'pose....Keep yourself clean and tidy and don't go drinking at the golf course...to excess anyway....Just behave yourself generally, and if you wish to misbehave, do it away from the golf and the golf course. – Fred "Bassett"

Positive attitude and communication skills. Excellent knowledge of golf and dedication to the job...and attention to detail. – Anonymous Caddy

You've always got to have confidence in your player and show your player that you've got confidence in them, because...they don't need...their caddy...looking...disappointed at the way things are going and looking...like a caddy who doesn't have trust in their player. I mean that's possibly the worst thing a caddy can do, I would have said. – Mike Patterson

I think all the good caddies can read their players' minds; can see what they're thinking. The best way...to describe how to be a good caddy is that you've gotta be able to put yourself in that person's shoes...to be able to see and...to think and...to look at the situation like you're in their shoes: 'What have they looked at?' 'How're they feeling?' 'What do they see?' – Steve Williams

Caddies need to keep an eye on the environment and their player at all times. For example, when a player goes to address the ball you need to be keeping half an eye on the wind (because it can change direction at any minute) and half an eye on the player, as they can get distracted or become hesitant and need to back off the ball and start again. As mentioned above, having a consistent pre-shot routine is essential for developing and maintaining confidence, not to mention producing a good shot!

As a caddy you can assist your player with this. Whilst the pre-shot routine is 100% within the player's control, it is easy to fool yourself. Players often try to tell themselves that they'll be fine ("crack on and let's play the shot"). However,

46

any distraction that a player experiences should not be ignored; instead, it should be acknowledged: the player should step away and re-group every time!

Remember, should your player need to step away, that doesn't mean that they necessarily have poor concentration; what it means is that they are disciplined! And as sport psychologists, we would rather see players who have good discipline than perfect concentration! So encourage your player to step away and regroup and start again with 100% concentration, confidence, and commitment.

> There's no point a player standing over a shot if they're not confident. Those are the sort of things you've got to look for. Sometimes you see a guy is not confident when they go play a shot, so you've got to read that into the situation. I mean, there is no point a player standing over a shot that he's not confident with. So if you sense he's not confident, you gotta...get him off and...talk about it, give him the confidence to do it....You'll know a player has certain situations and certain shots that he's not comfortable with and you know that and you know they're very important situations. – Steve Williams

If players are to approach a shot confidently they need to be confident in the ability of their caddy. This is all part of the trust building process. [See Chapter 4 where we discuss problems with trust as a barrier to achievement.] Some players like to retain a degree of control and carry their own yardage book and crunch the numbers at the same time as their caddy. One caddy recalls the time he caddied for a player at the Evian Masters who always carried a yardage book and did the yardages alongside her caddy's numbers. (This particular caddy stepped in as her usual caddy was unable to work that week.) After he made some good calls as to shot choice, she ditched her yardage book and relied totally on him. This was a complete sign of trust in him; moreover, he considered it particularly flattering as she never did that with her usual caddy.

If players are going to be confident in the chosen shot, and going to be 100% committed, they need to be able to trust and be confident in the yardages that their caddy gives them. This process may take a while, especially at the beginning of a relationship, and it's often wise for players to take a yardage book until they feel comfortable relying completely on their caddy. Some players may also have the philosophy that two heads are better than one and that it would be better for both of them to calculate the yardage so they can back each other up (if one was to make a mistake). Regardless of how players create their confidence in the chosen shot and club choice, they need to be 100% confident and committed or they are guaranteed to play their shot poorly. Confidence and commitment is crucial to a golfer's performance.

> You can't ever commit and put your best swing on it, if you're not sure about the club....By the time it comes to the decision, you both agree and you're like 'right let's produce a shot here'....Nine times out of ten she doesn't need it, but every now and again; like seventeen yesterday, we disagreed on a club and she took a seven iron out and just as she was in preparation, I say to her 'perfect club that, that's spot on'....Maybe it makes her feel better, maybe it doesn't, but...when she stands over the club...she thinks 'right.' As it turns out, she hit a beauty. One bounce and it was over the back of the green. – Mark Fulcher

> That's not always the case on each day, that the player is one hundred percent confident, but that's what most caddies aim to have: their player's complete confidence, even if it ends up being wrong....It's better to have a player trusting what their doing....Make sure they're standing over a shot knowing what they're doing is right...because I think golf's a game that's...based on confidence. – Mike Patterson

The time it takes players to trust their caddy, and their ability to do yardages, and advise on game plan tactics, green readings, and types of shot to play, can be shortcut by a caddy's experience, reputation, and previous observations by the player of the caddy in action. For example, if a caddy has been on tour for a long time, and has only worked for high performing players, he may have a reputation for being good and therefore the player may be inclined to trust him more quickly. Or if golfers have played in the same group as a caddy, when he was working for another player, and they've seen how he worked and how he interacted with the previous player on course, they maybe inclined to go in and trust him instantly. A caddy will help speed this process up as well if she makes a "good call" early on, where she may suggest a shot or club different to what her player thinks; the player goes with it and it turns out to be good. Convincing the player of this "good call" requires good communication skills, where you can effectively communicate your idea, backing it up with logical reasoning (see Chapter 2 for further detail).

> They have to have complete trust in your numbers and…your lines….If the caddy makes a good decision…that a player didn't necessarily think was the right decision at the start, and he hits the shot, trusts the caddy, it probably only takes one incident…where the caddy says 'no this is right, trust me,' and they do and it comes off. – Mike Patterson

> As soon as I get a number I'll know pretty much it's gonna be one of two clubs…and then I start thinking about why one club would be better than the other and…we talk all the way through about each shot….She'll ask me questions and…I'll ask her questions. – Mike Patterson

Ultimately the Player makes the Final Decision

Each time a player goes to play a shot she needs to own the shot. That is she needs to believe 100% in the club chosen and the type of shot she's going to play and her ability to pull it off. That's the definition of confidence! If she chooses this shot herself then she's more likely to believe that it's the correct choice. As the player is the boss, or the captain of the team, she is the ultimate decision maker. The caddy's role is to provide information (to persuade), but ultimately, it's the player's choice. There are different ways of doing this and every caddy has his way of doing it. Mark Fulcher and Steve Williams both have very different approaches to their caddying, but both allow their players to make the final decision:

> I'm of the...opinion that caddies should never tell a player what club it is....They should advise and...if she said 'seven'; instead of saying 'no I don't think so, it's six'...I always give a reason: 'well don't you think the wind's slightly into, perhaps?' or 'Are you

considering...?' And to be honest, I s'pose it's a bit of a cowardly way, but it's a way of making them think they make the decision....Because there is nothing worse as a player being told...I've done that in the past....Very few players, but some players like that....If you sometimes say 'seven, is this good?' Then the answer's got to be positive, not 'maybe,' 'could be.' 'Perfect club,' y'know. That's different. But when you're trying to change their mind, I always try and give them reasons why they should change their mind....Then they can think about it and if...my player agrees she will, if she doesn't she won't... With...my player the final decision is hers, it always has been. Rarely do I say 'absolutely not.' – Mark Fulcher

I give the player the yardage...and the necessary information that goes along with that yardage, and I tell them what I think...up front...I just think it gives the player a definite starting point, and the player knows you've thought about it, that you've given him that information, that you've obviously thought about it, and then it generally is giving you something to start with. Not like...'What do you think?' or How far do you hit...?' It shows that you've thought about it, you've come up with your thing. I think it's better for the player to have...somewhere to start with in their head. – Steve Williams

Great caddies will back the player's choice (no matter what their opinion at the end of the day), as they are both on the same team, and they want their player to perform to the best of his ability. Doing this in a manner that empowers the player is also a very clever way of building confidence. For example, Mark Fulcher's approach is very appropriate for caddies working with women golfers, as often women have lower self-confidence levels than their male counterparts, and this approach helps build their confidence and put the player clearly in the driver's seat. Steve William's approach is perhaps liked more by male golfers, as they generally prefer a no-nonsense business-like approach to the game and are comfortable and not threatened by their role as the boss in the relationship.

Mark Fulcher's empowerment approach uses suggestive questions. For example, he would give the facts first and foremost and then suggest "you could play it this way..." By suggesting one option, as if it were one of many, allows room for his player to suggest otherwise, and it gives him room to back the player's choice, even if it differs completely to his. Also by asking if she is thinking something is another way to subtlety reinforce and back her decision and or allow her to choose the idea he has given her, as if it was her choice in the first place. This approach can also work with men, too, but as a caddy you need to find firstly what works best for your player and secondly what suits your personality and style. [See Chapter 4 for more on personality matches.]

> Body language. You know when she fancies a hole and when she doesn't fancy a hole...it's the body language and the way she is being, the way she talks about the hole. Perhaps when she's on the tee, she'll stand there, and she's, instead of taking the driver...she might be thinking what to do. I think it's a judge of character...sometimes you get it right, sometimes you don't. But generally...you can ask her a question. If she stands there and then takes the driver out, you say 'well, you too thinking of taking three wood out?' or something like that...and I'll walk up to the tee. It happened in the last couple of weeks. I'm thinking three wood off this tee; it's not driver, like we did yesterday, and as we walk off the green, I can almost sense that she might be thinking the same, so I say...to her, 'you thinking what I'm thinking?' and if she says 'no,' I think 'well she's not.' She might say 'what?' I know, but chances are she'll say 'yeah I am. Three wood yeah?' – Mark Fulcher

Regardless of your approach, remember that the player's decision is final and requires your backing at all times, as this is the only way you can work together as a team and not undermine each other. Furthermore, it's the most effective way to get the player completely confident and committed for a shot.

> Sometimes...the players, they'll take like a five iron, and you're between the five and the six, and you don't want to hit it or commit. You must commit. Once you pull that club, it's the right club...even if it turns out to be the wrong one....You know you can pull it and half hit it, that's negative...You must be positive. Once you've committed yourself to a club, it's the right club. If it turns out a bit awful, that's just too bad; you made a mistake....You must be positive....The number of times you see players sort of half hit shots and make a mess of them because they don't commit! - Fred "Bassett"

We'd like to conclude this chapter with our decision making model. This is based on Lavallee et al.'s (2002) research with Australian PGA tour golfers and their caddies.

The first stage is about the player choosing a shot to play based on information available (how much of this the caddy will provide will depend on what the player is expecting).

In the second stage, the caddy considers whether he agrees or disagrees with the player. If they agree they will simply confirm the player's decision. If they disagree, and the caddy is in no position to advise the player to change, or if he is uncertain, Lavallee et al. (2002) found most caddies would go along with the player's choice. It was found to be important **how** the caddy went about communicating this. Caddies need to give their responses confidently and without hesitation, so that the player will not sense any doubt: Doubt or hesitation can be disastrous for a player's trust in a caddy and subsequent performance. If the caddy disagrees, she needs to provide more information on which the player can make a re-evaluation.

Finally, it is ultimately the player's decision on how to play the shot. Whatever the choice, the caddy needs to back the player, making sure that the player is both confident and 100% committed to that shot.

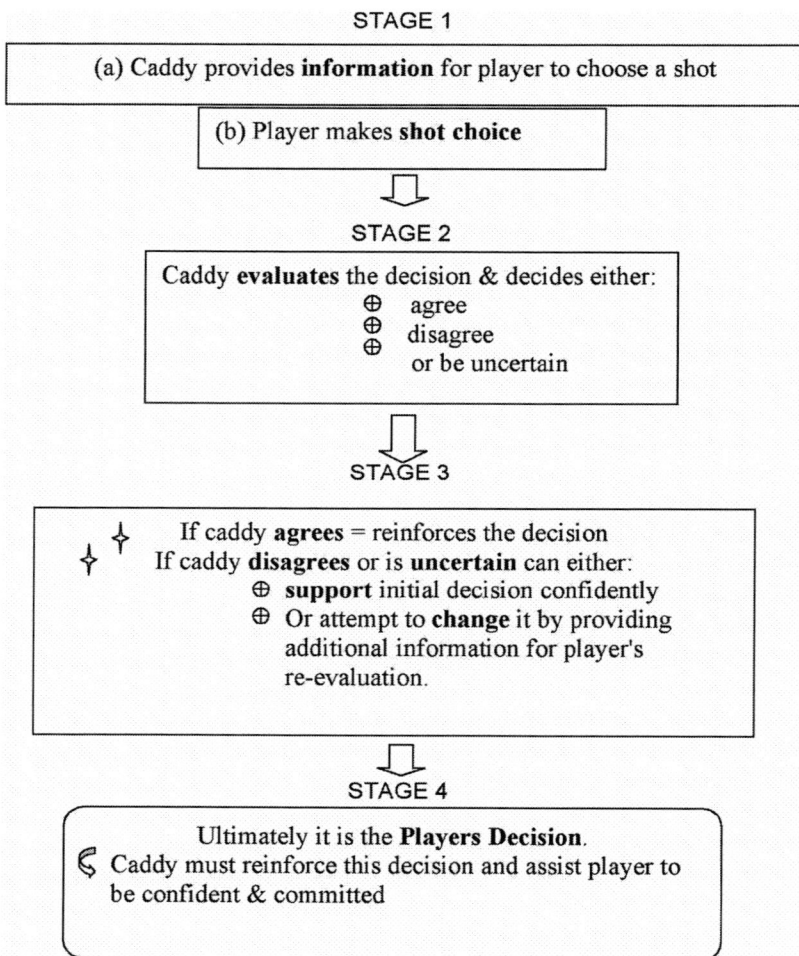

STAGE 1

(a) Caddy provides **information** for player to choose a shot

(b) Player makes **shot choice**

STAGE 2

Caddy **evaluates** the decision & decides either:
- ⊕ agree
- ⊕ disagree
- ⊕ or be uncertain

STAGE 3

If caddy **agrees** = reinforces the decision
If caddy **disagrees** or is **uncertain** can either:
- ⊕ **support** initial decision confidently
- ⊕ Or attempt to **change** it by providing additional information for player's re-evaluation.

STAGE 4

Ultimately it is the **Players Decision**.
Caddy must reinforce this decision and assist player to be confident & committed

Player-caddy decision-making model

How a caddy thinks and communicates to his player on the course is therefore supremely important in maintaining his player's confidence, especially when going through the shot decision-making process. [See Chapter 2 again for the caddy-talk process.]

54

Conclusion

In conclusion, the decision-making process requires many things. You must have a good game plan, set the right kind of goals, use consistent competition routines, have positive self-talk, and be confident in your choices. Furthermore, the process in which the player and caddy arrive at choosing their shot and club to play is most effective when the player is empowered as the final decision-maker and this is influenced strongly by a self-confident caddy.

What this Means for the Caddy

As a caddy, your aim is to exude confidence when conveying your decisions. This requires believing in your own ability, using positive self-talk, and focusing on your goals (especially process goals). Get to know your player and his reactions to varying situations so that you can respond accordingly. You also need to build good observational and communication skills so that you can watch and talk with your player to gain a clear understanding of his preferences.

What this Means for the Player

As a golfer, you need to have good game plans and clear goals, both motivational goals (outcome and performance goals) and process goals. Remember to focus more on process goals during a round and work on your performance goals mostly in practice sessions (let the outcome goals happen). Furthermore, you should communicate your goals to your caddy so that he knows what you want to achieve and can help you achieve your goals. Be sure you use your yardage book to your advantage; again, let your caddy help you. And don't forget to use consistent routines and other confidence-boosting activities to help get you into the zone. Finally, remember that the responsibility of the final shot and club choice is yours. Let your caddy help you choose your club and shot—remember, they may know you better than you think. However, whatever you decide to do, be confident that it is the best choice and then fully commit to it.

Reference

Lavallee, D., Bruce, D., Gorely, T., & Lavallee, R.M. (2002). *The golfer-caddie partnership: An exploratory investigation into the role of the caddie.* In E. Thain (Ed.), *Golf Science IV: The Proceedings of the World Scientific Congress of Golf* (pp.284-297). London: Routledge.

Chapter 4: BARRIERS TO EFFECTIVENESS
Know your role and know your golfer!

We hope that all of your caddy-player experiences are great. Unfortunately, we know they're not always the way you'd like them to be. There are many potential barriers to a successful relationship. In this chapter we'll address several of the most important ones: blaming the caddy for mistakes, not trusting each other, caddies having multiple roles, and personality differences.

Blaming the Caddy for Mistakes

As we described the caddy-player relationship in Chapter 3, caddies provide helpful input into the decision-making process. However, it's the player who makes the final decision. Therefore, it's wrong to blame the caddy for mistakes made by the player. Blaming the caddy never helps the relationship and when it happens it's a barrier to success!

Players who illogically blame their caddy for mistakes on a frequent basis can quickly undermine their caddy's confidence. If a caddy is not confident to speak his mind, a player will miss out on a crucial opinion, when it's needed the most. Caddies and players in this type of relationship need to sit down and discuss how they can better attribute poor performance (i.e., during a debriefing session). Regardless, caddies need to become fairly immune to emotional outpourings of their players in order that they can be confident.

> When...you're a caddy, you're obviously a sounding block...the guy takes out a lot of his frustrations; it's not directed at you, it's just his way of getting out his frustrations. They say things that...if you had a soft sort of personality, you took it to heart, you wouldn't last long as a caddy. You hear a lot of things that are said...they are directed at you, but they are not meant for you....When you're a caddy and you get directed some of the abuse that can be thrown at you, you just

close your ear, or it just goes in one ear and out the other, like you didn't hear it. – Steve Williams

Mistakes will be made! Through caddy-talk you'll discover what they were and how to correct them. Most caddies say they have learnt to do this by trial and error.

> I learnt something yesterday….Everyday you learn something different, because every situation's different…if you're in that situation again you can look back and think 'well we were in that situation and this is what we did and it was right or wrong or whatever.' If it was wrong, you have to make sure it's right the second time. – Mike Patterson

Trust

As we discussed in the last chapter, it's vital that golfers trust their caddies. When they don't, the decision-making process breaks down and a barrier to success exists.

Fortunately, trust can be developed. To begin with, you'll need to get to know each other really well (see below). The more you know about each other, the easier it will be to recognise each other's strengths and weaknesses. You'll therefore get to know the areas where it's easier to trust each other; you'll also be able to identify which areas need work.

> The most important thing between a player and caddy is trust, there's no question about that. I mean...the player has to have one hundred percent confidence that...the caddy is doing the best available job they can; then he never has to worry about him...Trust is the most important thing....You've got to go experience all the situations with a player...so he can see how you're gonna react under different situations. When...you go through all the different scenarios and he sees that you're the same person with a win, same with a hard loss, same when you're playing badly, same when you're playing well... in all different things, then he has complete trust. – Steve Williams

Once you begin your working relationship, you'll be able to develop your trust as you give advice, see the results of that advice, and debrief about what worked and what didn't work. Together, as a team, you'll develop trust in each other's ability as you experience different situations. As you continue your relationship over time, you'll develop this trust even more.

> It takes a little bit of time, as a player, to build up a certain amount of trust in your caddy....Once you've made a few good calls, then that's when players will start to trust you more; but obviously, if you're making a couple of mistakes, that's when that trust maybe starts to...go back just that little bit; but...it's your job to build that trust back up again. – Mike Patterson

Trust is also a two-way street. Not only does the player need to trust the caddy, but the caddy needs to trust the player. When mutual trust exists in the relationship, it's then possible to work as a synergistic team, where the sum of both parts is greater than the individual parts. In other words, when both caddy and player work together in complete trust, the resultant performance is better than if the player was on his own. A mutual team also has the possibility to be a lot of fun, too!

> The player's got the final call, but...I think they have to trust you a lot, too...listen to you when you're trying to stop them from doing something, where you think they're gonna make a mistake....You also have to trust your player that she knows too that...caddies make mistakes sometimes and...bring trouble into play and whatever, which doesn't need to be done. But the player can stop the caddy and that's when it works well together, when you can stop each other...making mistakes. – Mike Patterson

> I think it's really nice sometimes when you have a relationship where, like when I worked for one player...it's an absolute all team, an all on team effort....I feel me and my current player are getting closer to that. But she's a different person....One of my old players could be a fun time...'Come on mate, let's make this birdie, let's finish it.' – Mark Fulcher

Caddies with Multiple Roles

The role of "caddy" is very specific: Caddies carry a golfer's bag and give advice on which clubs to use. Of course, as you should be well aware by now, the job requires much more than that! As discussed throughout this book, caddies are sometimes psychologists, nutritionists, managers, etc. Furthermore, the realities of life mean that caddies are often parents, siblings, children, spouses, boy/girl friends, and/or best friends. When these situations happen, it's important that caddies realize these other roles can create important conflicts which may hurt the caddy-golfer working relationship. This also means that you must learn to manage these roles effectively, keeping them separate, and most importantly, doing what's best for your player!

The main reason that having dual roles (e.g., caddy and parent/spouse) may lead to conflicts may be obvious: it's about power. Each relationship has a power ratio: one person has more power than the other, or power is shared. In golf, the power should belong to the player. She should make all of the final decisions. She should decide which tournaments to play, which foods to eat, which types of exercises to do, which club to use, and which shot to hit. Other people should be there to provide advice, but ultimately it's the player's final decision. Or at least it *should* be!

If, however, there's a different power relationship, for example, the caddy is the golfer's parent, then, the power usually belongs to the parent (because that's true in all other aspects of the child's life: choices of sports to play, schools to attend, food to eat, etc.). This can therefore be a problem if the parent doesn't give up power to his child when carrying his bag.

This inappropriate power balance may mean that the communication process breaks down. Golfing children (and spouses, partners, friends, etc.) may be very reluctant to communicate openly and honestly when they believe their caddy has more power than they do. Moreover, if there is a tendency for arguments outside of golf, instead of effective communication, then there's a likelihood that arguments will erupt on the golf course, too.

This means that in order to overcome potential problems, it's important to remember that this relationship is unique. Everyone must realize his role, appreciate who's in control, and work to create the best possible environment for the golfer's success. To do this, those individuals who normally have the most power in this relationship have to give it up; the player must have the final say in what happens! This is not an easy strategy, especially when dealing with young children, but it is an essential strategy if success is to be expected.

Knowing your role and maintaining your role is vital. Sitting down together with your golfer/caddy and filling in the exercise on multiple roles will help you clarify this (see Appendix B4). Remember it's about empowering the golfer— part of building her confidence and self-belief as a golfer. And as we all know, confident golfers perform better.

Another issue that can arise with multiple roles is the concept of emotional involvement. If you are a parent, partner, or good friend of the player, you want your player to perform well. It becomes important to you, as you know that his performance will have an affect on him as a person and will therefore affect the relationship off the course. Working with a loved one may also bring other pressures which can exacerbate the caddy's feelings of emotional involvement, for example, when a caddy is working for her partner and her only income for the partnership is reliant solely on the player's performance. Like any other job, being a caddy requires a degree of professionalism where you are able to operate without letting your emotions get in the way.

I think if she's down, if she's having a bad day, yeah, absolutely; that's my job. I help to do everything I can to make her perform her best. If the caddy's head goes down, the players notice it very quickly....And I try, specifically; if she's hit a bad shot...to have a neutral reaction…it's very important, as they look at you. – Mark Fulcher

This is often easier said than done. The first author has seen many caddies working for loved ones express their emotions inappropriately on course. To huff, tut, or look disappointed at your player's poor performance will not help him play well. At all times you need to look like you believe that your player can turn it around and that this is merely a small blip in the round and you are confident in his ability to do so.

I think you just have to…be exactly the same all the time and…you've always got to have confidence in your player and show your player that you've got confidence in them, because… if they're struggling or whatever, they don't need to see their caddy…dragging along twenty yards behind them looking…disappointed at the way things are going and looking…like a caddy who doesn't have trust in their player. I mean that's possibly the worst thing a caddy can do I would have said. – Mike Patterson

Even caddies who've started jobs with players on a purely professional basis and had no multiple roles, can develop such good friendships that it can be difficult to turn the emotional attachment off when on course. If you cannot control your emotions on course, then it may be time to look for another job where there are no multiple role conflicts.

You know sometimes…you can work with somebody, you've been the best of friends off the golf course, but on a golf course it just doesn't work out, sometimes….Sometimes you can be too friendly…with them….I've been sacked many a time…not because I just wasn't doing the job. You just can be too close…or just not gelling….I think you have to like each other….You don't have to be…bosom pals or anything…because sometimes that's a hindrance, if

63

you're too close. You just need friendship and respect for one another. – Fred "Bassett"

That's one of the very important things I learnt…when I caddied for Greg Norman, that if you become too friendly with them they become like a job, and you do things you wouldn't normally do. You got to know…when you're working and when it's time to be serious and when it's not time to be serious. You've got to separate the friendship and the work. Hopefully you get to the golf course and…caddy for your boss, you're the caddy and it's time to get your head round it; that that's the way it is. – Steve Williams

Know Your Personality

To thoroughly understand your role, relative to your player's or caddy's role, you need to know everyone's personality. As we stated above, caddies should get to know their golfers as much as possible before starting a working relationship—the same is true in reverse: Golfers need to know the personalities of their caddies. Knowing what they like and dislike; knowing their definition of success (is it winning or setting personal bests?); knowing how they like to travel; knowing their favourite foods; knowing how much they like to joke around while playing golf; these are some of the things caddies and players need to find out before they start working with each other. What we're suggesting is that personality is very important for an effective working relationship. Specifically, having personalities that are more similar than different will enhance your relationship and make it work better; having a mismatch can be a barrier to success.

Unfortunately, it's not always easy to get to know someone before carrying her bag. Obviously, if you're working with a relative or close friend, this should be easier. If, on the other hand, you're working with someone you've never met before, you'll need to get to know her as fast as possible before you tee it up.

Getting to know someone quickly is a skill that you can learn. You'll need to spend some time with your new colleague before picking up the bag. Maybe having lunch together, or spending some time on the practice range and having a few practice rounds would be helpful.

What you'll want to do is find out what's expected of you as a caddy. Clarify the job description. Ask questions about your golfer's likes and dislikes, especially when practicing and playing. Ask questions about your role: Does he want you to give advice or just hand out clubs? Does she want you to help psych her up or calm her down? Does he want your help reading greens or just yardage and club choice? You'll also want to know if she likes to get up early, go to bed late, be at the club an hour (or whenever) before a match, eat before or after a round, have a drink (or two) after playing, etc. The more you know, the better you'll be prepared to deal with her preparation and results.

Different players need different things. Like my current player doesn't need my help on the greens. I don't...do that. It is added pressure on the job...so...you have to be pretty confident on the greens....They soon find out

65

who the good caddies are…and who are not. Like the job offers you get really, they want somebody who they can get on with; that is…most important. You might not be the greatest caddy in the world…but if you're good company…out there…that is worth…a lot. – Fred "Bassett"

Conclusion

In conclusion, being a caddy is about knowing what your role is, and knowing what it's not. Furthermore, it's important to keep roles separate. It's also about knowing your golfer, and building trust in your relationship. The more you're able to understand who you are, who you're working with, and what you're supposed to do, the better you'll be able to do it. However, no matter how good your relationship is, and how much trust you have in each other's decision-making, it's ultimately the golfer's decision to make—so don't blame the caddy if it's the wrong one!

What this Means for the Caddy

Caddies need to be sure they can work *effectively* with their golfers. To do so, you need to be sure there's a personality match. If there's a match, then most of the potential barriers to success rarely happen. Be sure you get to know your player as much as you possibly can before starting a relationship—if it's a good one, it may last a long time and you'll be very successful! However, be aware of any power issues that may negatively affect your ability to give good advice. If at all possible, don't take on more than one role. For example, instead of caddying for your partner, maybe it would be wiser to let someone else take on the job.

What this Means for the Player

Players also need to know their caddies well in advance of beginning a working relationship. It's not a good idea to just pick anyone at random and expect it to work. Also, keep in mind power issues. The player should always make the final decision. If there are power issues that prevent this, do something about it. Finally, your caddy needs to have the ability to control his emotions on course or he may quickly undermine your confidence and performance.

Chapter 5: SWITCHING OFF
Focusing your attention away from golf between shots

Throughout this book we've focused on the thoughts associated with achieving excellent performance. Sometimes, however, golfers need to think about something other than golf. It's impossible, *and not healthy*, to try to constantly think about strategy, goals, pre-shot routines, and the multitude of decisions that need to be made during a round.

In fact, most rounds of golf last for four hours or more—if you are involved with professional golf, the rounds are commonly five hours or more. Furthermore, if you shoot a score of 90, you would spend approximately two minutes actually hitting or striking the ball and one hour preparing to hit the ball (i.e., assessing shots and going through pre-shot routines). This leaves 2 hours 58 minutes of down-time between shots!

Many players—club-level, elite amateurs, and touring professionals, alike—try to think about their game between shots, whether it's about the shot they've just hit or their strategy for the next shot (or hole). Sometimes, these thoughts help performance (e.g., when planning for the next shot); however, in other cases, these thoughts hurt performance (e.g., when thinking so much about a bad shot that you are not focussed on your next shot). Ideally, what you'll do is **switch off** between shots, then **switch on** again when you start your pre-shot routine. The goal is to conserve energy and focus only when necessary. The caddy's job is to assist the golfer in this process.

The caddy also needs to switch off when walking between shots. Moreover, caddies need a little mental break between shots, too; they also need to be at their best when they need to switch on again and help make decisions. In this chapter we'll cover some techniques that caddies and players can use to help switch off, including conversation, games, music, and nutrition breaks. Furthermore, we'll discuss a couple of related issues (fitness and equipment management) because they also affect concentration. Finally, we'll finish this chapter by reminding you that sometimes caddies can look like their switched off, when they're really switched on.

Conversation

One way caddies can help their players to switch off and on is to use their caddy-talk. In other words, what you want to do is to change conversational topics back to the task at hand when its time to switch on. During the rest of the time, you can talk about anything else the player wants to talk about(preferably non-golf related stuff).

I know that ten, fifteen yards before we reach the ball it's time to start thinking about the shot. I will cut conversation off....Just before you get to the ball; that's when you have to start thinking about what you have to do about the next shot so...I often just say something...like...maybe you need to start concentrating now. – Mike Patterson

You need to switch off a little between shots....You don't want to be walking up to the ball thinking about your next shot; you do that when you get there. So if you can do, have a little bit of...small talk; not too much. You sort of learn...by experience when to...have a bit of small talk...a bit of a switch off for a little minute. Sometimes you don't talk, sometimes you keep away....You sort of learn that. – Fred "Bassett"

Of course, knowing your player and her interests away from golf can also provide for good conversational material. Many golfers like sport in general and this is often a common topic of interest. If a golfer and his caddy have similar interests this makes conversation relatively easy.

We've got similar interests...sports and stuff like...that sort of thing. I think...you gotta be more of a friend out there on the course than anything; that's the biggest thing, I reckon if you gonna caddy for someone you gotta be a friend with them as well....It's very important...you can't have chalk and cheese out there. – Anonymous Caddy

Furthermore, having a sense of humour can also be helpful, as this can not only serve as a good switch-off distraction for the player, but can also provide much often needed entertainment, especially when play is slow or if players and caddies experience rain delays (where even more downtime is passed in each others company).

When playing, we have a bit of a laugh...we have quite a few laughs, actually; she's good for that, and I think you need some sense of humour...most important to have a sense of humour...just to switch off for a couple of minutes and just relax. I think it does anyway. – Fred "Bassett"

As we indicated when describing process goals, golfers need to manage the things within their control, and switching off and on is definitely within your control. So, you should make this one of your goals and discuss the strategies you're going to use to achieve this goal. Of course, it's best if you work on this goal together; that way you can keep each other accountable.

Games

Another way to switch off is to play games. For example, one caddy and player combination told us that they picked an obscure word from the dictionary and used it in a sentence on each hole. Other games you could play include the following:
- Counting squirrels or birds in the trees.
- Picking pictures out of the clouds.
- Picking a topic or range of topics to discuss in advance.
- Playing rock, paper, scissors for deciding who will clean the club or other little tasks throughout the round.
- Playing for imaginary or real fans.
- Talking to fans/spectators.

All of these are fun ways to create conversational material. Be creative!

Music

A lot of golfers like to choose a song that they like and perhaps find inspiring to help them switch off between shots. Whilst actively listening to music on a personal music player (such as an MP3 player) is not allowed in competitions, golfers can still sing to themselves. If you've seen the movie

"Shawshank Redemption," in it the main character (played by Tim Robbins) has a music player taken away from him and he remarks that they can't take the music away from his mind and memory. If he can do it, so can you!

When choosing a song to sing to yourself, it is important to choose something that is either emotionally neutral or motivating. For example, to choose Beck's "Loser" song with the lyrics "I'm a loser baby, so why don't you kill me" is not going to help with your confidence! Obviously, what's motivational for one person isn't for another, so you'll have to choose what works for you. Furthermore, something motivational might make you too psyched up and unable to physically perform at your best. Therefore, for some people having something too motivational is a bad idea. You'll probably need to try out a few options until you find the one that works best for you. If you are stuck for ideas here are some examples of some motivational songs:

- "Hero" – by Mariah Carey
- "Superman" – by R. Kelly (from "Space Jam," the Michael Jordan movie)
- "Loyal" – by Dave Dobbyn
- "High" – by Lighthouse Family
- "Fly like an Eagle" – by Seal
- "Chariots of Fire" theme tune
- "World Looking In"– by Morcheeba
- "Eye of the Tiger" – by Survivor (from the "Rocky" movie)
- "Nothing's Gonna Stop us Now" – by Starship
- "Reach for the stars" – S Club 7
- "Simply the Best" – by Tina Turner

Alternatively you could choose a song that helps you to achieve your process goals such as:

- "Rhythm is a Dancer" – by Snap! (for help with "get up and go" and also rhythm.)
- "Turn the Radio Up" – by Barry Manilow (for encouraging positive self-talk and selected focus.)

- "When the Going gets Tough, the Tough get Going" – by Billy Ocean (for maintaining effort in difficult circumstances.)

Nutrition, Fitness, and Equipment Management

Another way to switch off is to take nutrition breaks. In order to perform at your best physiologically and psychologically, both caddies and players need fuel in the form of food and drink. Players and caddies who are dehydrated, or who have not replenished their sugar levels, will lose concentration. In order to maintain the ability to focus (especially towards the end of a round), players and caddies need to ensure they have plenty of water (and sports drinks which replace lost salts and minerals) and slow release energy foods (e.g., bananas or low fat oat bars or sandwiches) in their bag. In addition, taking the time to eat and drink allows you to switch off. Enjoy these breaks—don't think about game plans or the next shot—just relax!

Good caddies will ensure that there is plenty of water and food in the golf bag, not just for their players, but for themselves as well. Furthermore, all caddies need to be cardiovascularly fit. Specifically, you need to be fit enough to walk 36 holes in a day with at least 15 kilograms on your back.

If you are not fit and able to carry a bag around a course, then you are unable to work! Your body is an important and intricate part of your job as a caddy. This requires building up shoulder and back strength, and the requisite leg strength, to carry all this weight. Anyone wishing to become a caddy should gradually develop into being someone able to carry a tour bag. Start by carrying a light carry bag for 9 holes, then 18 holes, and then switch to a tour bag. In addition, you can develop your muscles through a variety of weight-training programmes that exist.

The caddy's job also involves keeping the clubs clean at all times because a player's performance will not be as good if the grooves of the club are dirty. The time it takes to clean a club is another opportunity to switch off. Great caddies, when off the course will also scrub their players' grips at least once a week (if it is hot they may need it more often) to prevent them from getting sticky, dirty, and/or shiny. Moreover, caddies need to have a wet towel to clean the golf ball, especially when it's on the green. All of these activities can be times to switch off.

The job gets a little more difficult in the rain, as caddies need to ensure that they have plenty of wet weather clothing for themselves and for their players. Specifically, they need to hold an umbrella over their players and keep the clubs, especially the grips, dry at all times. This requires keeping a cover over the top of the golf bag, too. You will need to take extra towels with you to help you keep the clubs dry and keep your player's hands dry. Carrying out these activities can serve as good switching off time. Again, be imaginative and think of ways to make these challenging situations as fun as possible!

My job involves making sure that everything is ready for play each morning. I make sure we've got enough balls, gloves, food in the bag and rain gear....I know what the weather forecast is and the wind direction...coz that way I have compass points in the yardage book....I'd rather carry...than forget the rain trousers. - Mike Patterson

There are a couple of additional things caddies need to know about their own equipment management. First, most professional golf-tour regulations require caddies to wear non-spiked or flat soled shoes; especially if they are to walk on the greens (this prevents further scuffing and damage to the greens). It is possible to buy waterproof trainers, but some caddies use waterproof golf shoes and cut the spikes off to flatten them (or unscrew them, if possible). If in doubt, check with the officials on your tour before choosing to wear them on course.

Second, many caddies who carry golf bags get themselves an extra strap—so that they effectively have a double strap—which allows them to carry the weight evenly on their backs. Some prefer just one ordinary strap. Choose the set up that works best for you.

Finally, most tour caddies prefer a normal tour bag to bags designed to go on a trolley (trundler or pull cart) or to a light carry bag, especially left-handers, as that way they can have the bag on their most dominant shoulder and leave their most appropriate hands free. Again, you decide what works best for you.

Looks can be Deceiving

It may look like a caddy's work is done when a player is over the ball; however, the best caddies will stay switched on when players are over the ball, so they can ensure their player is carrying out their routine properly, and that the circumstances in which they choose their shot doesn't change. Caddies need to stay alert until the ball comes to a rest!

When a player is playing, you've got to be constantly watching them...when he gets over the ball even. You've gotta be watching the conditions; the conditions can change quickly over the ball; inevitably it may, so get your player to back off the ball, even at the start of the shot....A lot of times you've gotta be paying attention to what the conditions are doing, they could change so quickly....A shot can go from upwind to downwind; you've got to be really aware of that and not be afraid to tell the player to get off the shot. Sometimes you're right, sometimes you're wrong. You've always gotta go with your instinct. – Steve Williams

Conclusion

Golfers and caddies need to switch off between shots in order to conserve energy so that they can effectively focus on all that they need to when addressing the ball. There are several ways that this can be achieved, from singing songs to oneself to employing games to distract the player. Keeping well fed and watered can also help keep concentration and can serve as a further distraction when used at the right time. Caddies and players need to switch on when it is time to play the shot and control over this is the responsibility of both the player and the caddy.

What this Means for the Caddy

Caddies, you should take an active part in helping your players switch off between shots. You can do this by engaging in conversation about non-golf topics, encouraging your players to sing to themselves, actively playing games with them, or taking a break to eat or drink. In order to help your player switch on and off, you need to learn his pre-shot routine and when and how he best likes to switch on and off. To do this you'll need to have both keen observational skills and the ability to communicate well with your player (i.e., you'll need good caddy-talk!).

What this Means for the Player

As a player, you need to switch off between shots, because you can't effectively concentrate for four to five hours. You will play better when you relax and switch off and think of non-golf related things between shots. You can sing to yourself, talk with your caddy or playing partners, or distract yourself with a number of games. Taking time to eat and drink can also serve as natural distractions. Planning what you will think about or do to distract yourself from your game between shots is essential, especially if this is not easy for you. When setting your goals for the round, make this one of your process goals and communicate this to your caddy— let him help you achieve this goal! Having a clear pre- and post-shot trigger (or point in which you start and finish your pre-shot routine) will also help you identify when to switch from off to on and vice-a-versa. There are lots of ways you can try and achieve this. Practice a few and find one that works best for you.

Chapter 6: CONCLUSION
What have we learned and what's next?

To conclude our book on caddy-talk, we need to review what we've suggested is good practice for caddies and golfers. We also need to recommend the next step in your development.

What Have we Taught you?

We set out in this book to teach you how to become a better caddy. Specifically, we wanted to inform you about how the science of psychology coincided with the experiences of expert caddies.

We started the book by focussing on the communication process (i.e., caddy-talk) because it's the life-blood of the caddy-golfer relationship. It's about turning the caddy's self-talk into persuasive communication. It's about providing players with helpful information—information needed to help players achieve their goals. The key to effective communication is knowing how to send messages that are received the way you want them to be received. To do this, you need to know some of the problems associated with sending and receiving effective messages—so we gave you some helpful tips.

In Chapter 3, we provided information on good decision making. Good decisions require having a good game plan and good goals. If you have a good game plan and appropriate goals, you should be confident you'll achieve them. This means having positive self-talk and using effective competition routines (especially a systematic pre-shot routine). We also made some suggestions for ways to increase your confidence, beyond what you can get from attaining your goals. These included acting confident, thinking confidently, and realising why you should feel confident (why you're a great caddy/player!). We finished this chapter by reminding you that no matter how successful caddies are at influencing their players, it's ultimately the players who make the final decisions—they have to live with those decisions.

We also pointed out that there are potential barriers to success in Chapter 4. We discussed blaming the caddy for mistakes, not trusting the caddy, caddies having multiple roles, and poor personality matches. Fortunately, we also suggested these potential problems can be overcome by getting to know each other before working together and being clear on everyone's role on your team.

The last chapter was about switching on and off. We wanted you to know that it's impossible to be "on" the entire time you're on the course. You can't concentrate all the time—in fact, you don't want to focus all the time! What you want to do is know when to start your pre-shot routine, and know what to do the rest of the time to switch off. We suggested a few things you could do, like playing games, talking about non-golf things, singing to yourself, or taking a nutrition break. Obviously, it's up to you to think of what works best for you, but you must think of something that will allow you to shut down between shots.

What's Next?

Okay, now that you're more aware of the psychology of being a golf caddy, what should you do next? We suggest you read more about sport psychology, in general. Or maybe attend a lecture on the topic. A great idea would be to attend a caddy training course (e.g., Caddie Connect in St. Andrews, Scotland). There's so much more you can learn. Alternatively, spend some time on-line; seek out ideas that seem relevant for you.

Finally, and most importantly, you need to experiment. If you try something you've learned (in this book or elsewhere) and it doesn't work, try something else! There's no "right" way. There's no "wrong" way. The best way is the way that works for you. Keep on trying until you get it the way you want it.

Whatever you do, we wish you all the best in your golfing future!

Appendix A: CASE STUDIES

Case Study 1: STEVE WILLIAMS

Currently works with Tiger Woods.
Others players he's worked with on the U.S. PGA Tour
include Ian Baker-Finch, Greg Norman, and Ray Floyd.

How Did You Get Into Caddying?

A: *Well I'd been interested in golf the whole time since I was
a kid, and my father was a top amateur at Paraparaumu
Beach Golf Course near Wellington [New Zealand]...and
there's the Caltex Open...which was a regular event back
in the seventies...and he got to play in the Caltex a
couple of times and when he was coming up to play, he
asked if I could come and caddy for him, which I could
and that's how it all started....All the top players used to
play in it...Peter Thomson, Kel Nagel, John Lister, Bob
Charles; they all played in it....I was thirteen years old [at
the time].*

Summary

Steve started young and always wanted to be a caddy. He
never had any intentions to play golf; rather it was the call of
a "bag man" for him. Steve has now been a professional
caddy for 28 years for some of the world's best male golfers
at the peaks of their careers, including the current world
number one, Tiger Woods.

Getting Hired

A: *I've been very fortunate that all...of the jobs I've had [have]
come to me. I got to work for Ian Baker-Finch starting
out...and while caddying for Ian...we were paired with
Greg Norman. He obviously liked what I was doing and
he gave me a call one Christmas to caddy for him....That
was alright; and then I went on from there. After finishing
with Greg, I was approached by Ray Floyd [and] caddied
for him; and then got approached by Tiger Woods. But*

I've…never had to go out and actually look for a job,
fortunately.
Q: Do you ever research a player prior to taking on his bag?
A: Nah, I mean I don't think you need to…when you're a
caddy; the only thing you need to know is how they
play….But I didn't, no.
Q: So you knew about these players before you took them on
anyway, because of their status.
A: Oh yep.

Summary

Steve's reputation became synonymous with the level of
players he was caddying for and therefore his players have
always come to him. Similarly, Steve knew a lot about his
players and the way they played prior to taking on their bags.

Getting Fired

A: I've only ever…got fired from Greg [Norman] and the
reason being that…I got too friendly with him…and I
stepped over the ground of being a friend and a caddy. At
the time I didn't…know I was doing it because…I got so
friendly with Greg…a lot of times I would overstep the
boundaries of being [a] caddy and [I was instead] being a
friend and not a caddy. Hence, the relationship went a bit
sour, so Greg fired me, which was no problem. And then I
obviously left Ray to caddy for Tiger, so I've only…been
fired once, from Greg, but as I said it was a great learning
experience….I learnt a lot which…helps me today, no
question about it. If I hadn't of caddied for Greg first up I
would never have got to where I am today. I learnt so
much caddying for him.

Summary

Steve got into caddying young. Jobs came to him as his
reputation grew alongside the calibre of players he worked
for. Being fired is often part of the tenuous caddy-player
relationship. Being fired from Greg Norman turned out to be a

great learning experience as it helped Steve clarify his role as a caddy.

Relationship Between Player and Caddy: Trust is Crucial to the Effectiveness of the Relationship

A: *The most important thing between a player and caddy is trust, there's no question about that. I mean...the player has to have one hundred percent confidence that...the caddy is doing the best available job they can; then he never has to worry about him...Trust is the most important thing....Most players, when they hire a caddy...they're gonna typically hire someone they already know they can trust. They've seen them work for somebody else. They've had a good relationship with somebody else, one that hasn't worked out for one reason or another. So they['ve] got an appointment that they already know they can trust. But...a player...has to go through the highs and the lows and they see how a caddy reacts to all these situations before he knows a hundred percent what a caddy is like. So...you've got to experience the victories, you've got to experience the hard life...all those. It takes a while before a player and [a] caddy have a pretty good understanding, so I think you've got to share all the experiences that go along with being a professional golfer....You've got to go experience all the situations with a player...so he can see how you're gonna react under different situations. When...you go through all the different scenarios and he sees that you're the same person with a win, same with a hard loss, same when you're playing badly, same when you're playing well...in all different things, then he has complete trust....A player has a lot to think about all the time...so when it comes to choosing the club selection, that more time...a player and caddy spend together you realise that the caddy's...always thinking what club, whatever....The more time you spend together the more trust you have [from your player] and he will rely more on your instinct.*

Q: Do you think that's good for the player to rely totally on the caddy's instincts?

A: I don't feel you should rely a hundred percent [on a caddy], cause a great...pair, a great team of caddy-player, I think ninety percent of the time they will be thinking the same thing.

Since Steve has always worked with his players for long periods of time he has always had the opportunity to develop trust:

A: I pride myself on doing the job the best I can and gaining a hundred percent trust with the player I work for, so I wouldn't even question it, I would say there is a hundred percent trust in each other.

Summary

Steve believes that players will only hire people they know they can trust. However, sealing that trust in the relationship involves time, where you experience the good and hard times together. Gaining your player's trust is important and it's done by putting in time and effort. Steve believes that when a player truly trusts his caddy he will use the caddy's advice more often.

Friendship Versus Business

A: When you caddy for someone you spend more time with that person than any other person does...you become really friendly...so you have to always...know when it's time for work and when it's not time for work....That's one of the very important things I learnt...when I caddied for Greg Norman, that if you become too friendly with them they become like a job, and you do things you wouldn't normally do. You got to know...when you're working and when it's time to be serious and when it's not time to be serious. You've got to separate the friendship and the work. Hopefully you get to the golf course and...caddy for your boss, you're the caddy and [it's] time to get [your head] round [it]; that that's the way it is.

Q: Do you become friends with them?

A: I think it's just because you spend so much time with that person....If you caddy for a player and he plays thirty *weeks a year...that's six days a week for thirty weeks of the year, eight hours a day sorta thing; you almost have to become friends, there's no way that you can't become friends because you spend so much time [together]. If a player sees you put a lot of effort and a lot of trust into it, then that is part of what a friendship involves. So you definitely become friends; but it's very important to distinguish between when it's time to be friends and when it's time to be an employee....I've only ever...got fired from Greg, and the reason being that...I got too friendly with him...and I stepped over the ground of being a friend and a caddy.*

Q: When you say you got too friendly with him, did you get emotionally involved?

A: Sort of...when you're a caddy and you get directed some of the abuse that can be thrown at you, you just close your ear [or] it just goes in one ear and out the other, like you didn't hear it. But coz I...got so friendly with Greg a lot of the times he would have some of his comments for me, that...he wasn't meaning anything [by them], but I'd fire right back at and...that wasn't something you should...do; but like I said I learnt a lot from him.

Summary

Becoming friends is inevitable as a caddy and player, according to Steve. However, as Steve learnt the hard way: it's crucial to know when you are working (and all business) and when you are just friends. Remembering that your professional relationship takes precedence over your friendship at all times is important in the success of your work together.

Working on Game and Course Management Plans is a Big Part of the Relationship

Q: Do you and the players that you work with ever set goals or, more specifically, make a game plan together prior to going out to play...on a daily basis?

A: Absolutely, I mean you gotta…and the more your player
progresses [through the tournament], the more you know
what he's going to do…we definitely talk about
things….We both…want to be on the same page….We
don't want one…who literally thinks the idea today is
twelve under par, that's gonna be the score that's gonna
win the tournament, when [the other] one of you thinks
ten under par's going [to] win….You both want to have a
fairly good idea what the winning score is and therefore
you know what you got to achieve and whether you're
going to play aggressive or defensive sort of thing. So
that's something you've both gotta discuss and agree
on….When you come to the last few holes of a
tournament you know you generally gotta have an idea
what the winning score's going to be. Now…if you're two
or three behind and it comes…to a hole, you've got a
fairly difficult hole that you play conservatively normally,
you're going to have to play aggressively in order to try
and make the birdies….So…I think one of the most
important things…when you are a caddy, is to look at the
last three or four holes of a tournament and how you're
going to play those holes (a) if you've just got a tie and
your leading, (b) if you're two or more ahead, or (c) if
you're behind [and] what sort of game plan you gotta to
look at that stage for.

The caddy needs to take into consideration what state his
player is in and what effect this will have on the game
plan for the day:

A: When the guy gets to the golf course and he's on the
range. 'Is he swinging good today?' Or 'is he not
swinging good today?' Y' know, can you see he's
confident today or he's a bit 'ify' today? But absolutely a
must….No good trying to go to the first hole and pull off a
miracle shot when you know the guy's not swinging good
or you've spoken to him or you've just seen it on the
range….If you [as a player] experience a difficult day,
you're not feeling well, or you don't feel strong…you're
weak or… y'know, all the different variables, you definitely
have to read that in. You [as the caddy] can't ask the guy
but you've got to read that in.

This is not necessarily something you discuss with your player rather you take your observations into consideration when discussing the tactics of the day.

Summary

Steve suggests that discussing and communicating your thoughts of the day's plan of attack is crucial in helping you work together as a team. This includes adapting the plan to the player and situation on the day, so that you know in advance, for example, how you will play the last three holes of the tournament.

Adapting to Different Players and Learning About Their Personalities

A: I think my first long-term relationship with Greg Norman…I would describe that as a great learning experience; we had a great time. I was very young at the time…I learnt a lot….Then I went to Ray Floyd, which was going from a young player to an older player…with a completely different outlook on life….[Ray was] obviously a family man, with three kids and…an established sort of player on tour and a whole different game as well; and then to go from Raymond to Tiger…a single guy…with boundless amounts of talent and enthusiasm and drive of the game. So, sort of three different stages really….That's what a caddy does, I mean…you just adapt and like it doesn't…take a long time, but it takes a little time just to figure out all the little things the player likes. Every guy has his own little things that he likes [and] dislikes; you gotta learn all those little things….Once you've learnt all those you're away….You generally get a fair idea of the player that you're working with, how their going to react in that situation and they [do] typically react the same way most of the time. So in your mind, know how someone's going to react, and then you've got to react how you know that player likes it to be reacted to; so it's simple.

Q: So you believe that a player will tend to be fairly predictable in the way that he reacts; is that what you're saying?

A: *Oh, I think if you work with somebody long enough yes, I think that a player will agree with you.*

Q: Okay, so you've got to learn those traits and then kind of stick by those rules that they set?

A: *Yeah.*

Summary

As a caddy, Steve has worked with players at different stages of their lives and with different personalities. Steve's adaptability, combined with spending both time, observation, and putting himself in his player's shoes, has helped him learn to judge his players' characters effectively.

Confidence and Commitment of Your Player

Q: How important is it to you that you make sure your player is confident before playing a shot?

A: *It's a hundred percent important. There's no point a player standing over a shot if they're not confident. Those are the sort of things you've got to look for. Sometimes you see a guy is not confident when they go play a shot, so you've got to read that into the situation. I mean, there is no point a player standing over a shot that he's not confident with. So if you sense he's not confident, you gotta…get him off and…talk about it, give him the confidence to do it….You'll know a player has certain situations and certain shots that he's not comfortable with and you know that and you know they're very important situations.*

Q: And if you detect any lack of confidence you'll pull him off the shot and talk to him about it?

A: *Exactly…I mean if you're going out there [as a player] and you ain't confident…with what you're doing, then you don't have trust in your ability; well its not going to do you any good. There's tonnes of guys out there that have*

*confidence and trust in their ability, you gotta be a
hundred percent confident.*

Q: Do you see it as part of your role as a caddy to increase a player's confidence?

A: *Absolutely...when a guy is going along and...he's got the biggest confidence, swinging well and all that...you do...take more aggressive lines or it's typical to play a little more aggressively. You've gotta talk about their confidence yourself 'hey you're swinging good' and things or whatever it is....You've gotta be able to read when a guy is confident and when he's not confident.*

Q: Do you think the ability to be able to read a person's confidence is crucial in your ability to be successful as a caddy?

A: *Absolutely....I think all the good caddies can read their players' minds; can see what they're thinking. The best way...to describe how to be a good caddy is that you've gotta be able to put yourself in that person's shoes...to be able to see and...to think and...to look at [the situation] like you're in their shoes: 'What have they looked at?' 'How're they feeling?' 'What do they see?'*

Q: How important is it to you to make sure your player is completely committed to his shot?

A: *Hundred percent; it's the same thing. You can detect, you can sometimes see a player standing over a shot [and] you can detect they're not feeling comfortable....There is nothing wrong with saying 'hey get off it, y'know, re-think what you're trying to do,' that sort of thing....You might come across a particular shot where you know the player is not comfortable, you know, you remind them, 'hey you've hit this shot a hundred times, a thousand times on the practice range; you know how to do it, this is no different [a] situation.' Block out the situation [and] make that same swing that you do on the practice range and go ahead.'*

Summary

A player needs to be confident if he is going to perform successfully. So Steve believes it is his role to help his players to keep confident and committed on every shot. This involves detecting any lack of confidence and commitment and pulling your player off his shot and building his confidence with positive affirmations going into a shot where necessary.

Maintaining Your Player's Confidence in the Long-Term

A: I'm a great believer that once every week finishes, [the] next week is a brand new week and there is no thought of the previous week. I'm a firm believer in that…if you've had a poor week, you start off the next week, have a good round and get the confidence going….I don't believe in changing things over [the] long haul, [only the] short haul. Once each round has finished and once each week has finished that is it. You might want to discuss it for ten minutes on the practice fairway afterwards, once that's it, it's all finished. You're looking forward to the next day…you don't dwell on the past. Golf's a sport that you certainly don't dwell on the past; I mean you go to the next tournament; you go through the same routine and know that you trust your ability and get off to a good start hopefully and your confidence rises.

Q: If you believe that, does the player believe that too?

A: Well you've gotta try and make them….You've gotta put bad stuff behind you…you gotta continue when things don't go well; okay you got a bad break…you've gotta put that behind you.

Q: Do you see it as your responsibility to make the player believe that it's a brand new week and you're putting everything behind you?

A: And that thing's are going forward, yes. You gotta…harp on a bit…'Thing's are gonna change.' You've gotta be very positive always, that's the hard part of it. Sometimes it hard to be positive; we all know that you go through bad patches…but that's the really important role of a caddy: to always be positive to try and install positive thoughts into the player's [mind so] that things can turn around.

91

Summary

As a caddy, Steve believes that you have to help your player move forward, forget about the past week and help him build his confidence going into the next week. Being positive is an important role of a caddy, especially when dealing with a player who may not be playing as well as he would like.

Role of a Caddy

Q: What are your responsibilities generally, as a caddy?
A: *To look after the golfer on the golf course....We all have the same responsibilities; we've all gotta be at the course to get the information, look after the golf clubs....As a caddy, your responsibilities are...just to get the yardages, and locate the pin positions, and...get a feel for what the golf course is playing like today....It's not really a responsibility, it's part of your job.*

The Caddy is to be the "Rock" of Emotional Support and Optimism for the Player

Keeping your head up and looking positive, in spite of whatever your player is doing, is important:
A: *Ultimately, the tough situation for a caddy is when you are going through the low situation, when you keep your head up...keep giving positive confidence from the bad situation....That's when a player has more respect for you when he sees, he obviously knows he's struggling a bit, but it doesn't work if he's struggling and he looks over to his caddy and his caddy's got his head down and he thinks it's over as well....Give the best that you can on all situations....If they're down or the guy's not playing well, our job is to help these guys play good but if they're not doing so good they can get down....That's the most important part: not to get down, to stay upbeat.*
You also need to be a motivator by being optimistic and positive about everything:
A: *If things go badly...you've got to point out that there's so many holes to go and you can knuckle down and make X*

amount of birdies or get those shots back or 'hey you've just got to forget that situation; you were unlucky' or 'y'know, we made a mistake' or 'that was a bad break; we've got to get over it we've got...how many holes left in the tournament we're still not out of it' or what ever it might be.

Q: Caddies out there [on the Ladies European Tour]...sometimes will bag their players....What're your thoughts on that kind of behaviour?

A: *Get another job...you've gotta remember one thing when you're a caddy, and I know exactly what you're saying, and I see it here [on the U.S. PGA Tour] all the time...you have to realise, as a caddy, [that] the person you're carrying the clubs for is trying a hundred percent on every shot. They're not trying to three putt, they're not trying to hit [it] in the water, they not trying to hit it out of bounds, they're not trying to hit it there; they're trying one hundred percent....I see that carry on all the time that's very negative and...that sort of thing won't last very long.*

Q: No it'll get back to the player eventually.

A: *Absolutely, I mean you can see it on the tee, you can see it on the guys...a player can see it in a guy's attitude and in the way the guy's acting....I understand if...your player's not giving a hundred percent, but then you are entitled to comment...about the negative things. But of all the guys I've caddied for, I've known that every time they've hit the shot they're giving it one hundred percent and you've gotta realise that they're trying as hard as they can, giving effort like most players.*

As a caddy you also need to be impervious and have the ability to weather whatever emotional rubbish your player may throw at you:

A: *On the golf course, when...you're a caddy, you're obviously a sounding block...the guy takes out a lot of his frustrations, it's not directed at you; it's just his way of getting out his frustrations. They say things that...if you had a soft sort of personality, you took it to heart, you wouldn't last long as a caddy. You hear a lot of things that are said, y'know, they are directed at you but they are not meant for you. When I got too friendly with Greg [Norman] and he would say well things for fun, and I'd answer right back in a fashion that I shouldn't have.*

Summary

An important part of Steve's job is to keep his head up at all times. Steve believes most players are not playing poorly on purpose; therefore you have to act accordingly and remember you're both on the same team! Weathering what a player might say as an emotional reaction is done by remembering it's not meant for you—it's not personal.

Caddy "Homework"

A: *I think a very good player would know when a caddy is not trying his hardest or would know [if] he hasn't done his homework properly. I think…all the best players are very alert, they're very… switched onto the game. Obviously they would know when a guy is not putting enough effort in or not.*

Q: What exactly is homework for a caddy?

A: *It's a matter of…go[ing] out on the course…and have a good look at the course….You see a lot of caddies…they just buy the yardage book these days and they've been here last year and they don't go out. They walk around the course in a practice round with a player. But go out there and make sure you scout the course properly. Prior to your round, starting and time permitting, [ensure] that you go out and look at HOW the course is playing, how the greens are, 'are the greens soft?' How the pin positions are today. At certain events…particularly the British Open…you are actually allowed to go out and…walk on the course, a lot of courses won't allow you to walk on them….Little things like that. Anything that you can do, that you think you might be able to get an edge [with], you want to do.*

Q: What can you do if you can't walk on the course itself?

A: *Obviously, you can still walk outside the ropes…you can't walk on the course; but certainly, every morning you go round and walk outside the ropes, time permitting….You can go…see where the pin positions [are]….You know where it is roughly from the diagrams…where they draw the green, but you actually know exactly in your mind [if you've walked the course]…you know exactly where the pin is so that the player knows when you put the dot low on the green: its right here its two yards left of this, three right of that, whatever…so you know exactly where it is.*

Summary

Good players know if you've done your homework as a caddy—it'll come across in your ability to confidently say where the pin is located, for example. Steve recommends that any edge you can give your player can only benefit the working relationship and ultimately your player's performance.

A Caddy is Constantly Thinking, Watching, and "Mind Reading"

Reading your player is important:

A: *The best way I can describe what a caddy does, or how I think it's best that a caddy does [his job], a caddy, he has to be able to put himself in that guy's shoes. And he has to feel that he's actually standing, when they're standing there on the fairway looking at approaching a shot, the caddy has to think he's actually standing in that guy's shoes knowing that they're going to be playing aggressively [or] if they should be playing defensively. 'Is he swinging poorly today?' Or [is he] 'swinging well today?' 'What sort of shot does he need to hit here?' 'What sort of shot can he hit here?' 'Is he nervous?' 'Is he not nervous?' 'What are we looking at?' As a caddy, think those things like he's standing in that guy's shoes; you'll get it right most of the time.*

Q: They're the kind of questions you would ask yourself each day when you go out to play?

A: *Absolutely…when the guy gets to the golf course and he's on the range.*

95

Q: Do you think the ability to be able to read a person's confidence is crucial in your ability to be successful as a caddy?

A: *Absolutely….If I was to put it in a nutshell, I think the best caddies can read their player's minds…..Like when I'm caddying…I know what sort of shot the player's gonna hit…so [I] give the guy the yardage and tell him 'look it's this'…this particular sort of shot…what you need to do, [you] need to hook in there to the pin, hold it, fade it, hit it high, hit it low, or whatever it might be….Every caddy has to be…able to see it standing in his [player's] shoes; [he] has to be able to see and feel what he's trying to do. And the more you handle players, the more you'll be able to do that, and once you can do that, you'll have a good opportunity to have a real good relationship with a player because it'll become second nature.*

Steve will never switch off even when his player is over the ball:

A: *I mean communication is a huge thing…and I think when a player is playing, you've got to be constantly watching them…when he gets over the ball even. You've gotta be watching the conditions; the conditions can change quickly over the ball; inevitably it may, so get your player to back off the ball, even at the start of the shot….A lot of times you've gotta be paying attention to what the conditions are [doing]; they could change so quickly….A shot can go from upwind to downwind; you've got to be really aware of that and not be afraid to tell the player to get off the shot. Sometimes you're right, sometimes you're wrong. You've always gotta go with your instinct….Top caddies always think of…what's happening next. 'What's the next hole?' 'How's that hole playing?' 'Where's the wind blowing there?' 'What's the firing hole?' Always thinking, 'how's the player?' 'How's he swinging today?' 'How's he gonna play this hole today?' 'What sort of shot's he gonna hit?' He's always thinking….You['re] not just out there carrying the clubs and giving the yardage. You're always thinking. I think the guys that are good caddies are always thinking ahead.*

Summary

Steve believes that watching and observing and knowing your player inside out allows you to eventually "mind read" him so that you can predict the kind of shot that he is thinking about. In order to do this, a good caddy like Steve will stay alert and constantly think ahead and will keep an eye on both the player and the weather conditions while they play a shot.

Communication: It's Important to Switch on for Your Shot and off Again Afterwards

A: *The moment...the player and caddy get to the ball...whatever they were talking [about] is finished, and its just full concentration [that] goes to that next shot that's hit; once it's hit your walking down the fairway, relax, and talk and joke or whatever it might be until you get to the next shot....Each person that you deal with has a different character and would have a different idea when it's time to be serious or not. So you have to determine that all, that's your own judgment.*

Talk Between Shots

A: *Obviously, in golf you want to keep the player's mind away from what he is doing as much as you can, except for when he's gotta come and hit the shot....Every caddy-golfer relationship is different....The common factor would be sport. Guys love to talk about sports...professional golfers love their sport, and all the other sports, so there's a lot to talk about sports and different things but...yeah, common denominator with sports people would be talking about sports; you've got to try talk about all aspects.*

Q: If things are going well in a round, what kind of things would you say to your player? What kind of conversations would you have?

A: *That's a question you get asked a lot. It's a very difficult question to answer, because every day it's different....I mean basically in a nutshell...when you're caddying for somebody you're trying to keep them loose and relaxed and obviously you want…them to have their mind off what their doing in between shots, so that they can focus solely…on each shot…that thirty seconds before each shot or whatever… the routine is that takes you through that shot; you want to focus as hard as you can. Then, in between, when you're walking down the fairways, walking to the tee…you want to…not be sorta stressed about the game, just enjoy what you're doing. So yeah, it's very hard to say what you talk about because there are so many things every day; you're in so many different situations and everything, they're so different.*

Shot Choice Information Processing and Communication

In order to be fully prepared for a shot, a caddy has to process a lot of information; however, Steve is careful in what and how he tells his player this information:

A: *When you're a caddy, [and] you get close to the ball, you're already in your head got a rough idea how far it is, you think…'what is going to be approximate' and what club you're looking at sorta thing….As you get closer to the yardage, as your walking up there, I'm already thinking what club it is, what sort of shot it is. If it's an exact number, I know I tell them first, I mean that's the way I do it and then he'll say 'yeah I agree with that' or 'maybe this' or whatever, but that's how I do it….If I give you a yardage and say whatever club…you're obviously not going to be more than one club off, so already you have sorta set what you think is it and then you can…say 'well do you think it's this?' 'Can I hit this club that far?' Or, 'Do I need one more?' [that] sort of thing. I just think it gives the guy a good base…to start with…. I probably do it different to most people….Whenever I've caddied, I give the yardage…of how far it is; all the info he needs there, and I tell him what I think it is, and let him come back to me….Ninety percent probably do it the other way round…where the caddy gives the information and the player does what they think is right or whatever….I've very seldom…have a player say 'What do you think?' I always tell them what I think. [I] give the player the*

98

yardage…and the necessary information that goes along with that yardage, and I tell them what I think…up front….I just think it gives the player a definite starting point, and the player knows you've thought about it, that you've given him that information that you've obviously thought about it, and then it generally [is] giving you something to start with. Not like…'What do you think?' or 'How far do you hit..?' It shows that you've thought about it, you've come up with your thing. I think it's better for the player to have…somewhere to start with in their head….I don't think you need to have that much information. I think you can give too much information. I believe in just very basic information….Obviously, you play not just for the heck of it; I would feel [it] is just as important [to gain their confidence] as what you're feeding them….A lot of people have different approaches as to what sort of information that's required. Some players like more information than others. But…golf is a game of feel and changes position….Personally I don't believe in giving lots and lots of information….A lot of players and caddies that you watch…they'll calculate each shot as X amount uphill or X amount downhill or take off this amount for wind, or this sort of thing, but…it's feel. I'd rather just give the yardage and say it's this much or it's downwind…so it make[s] it more of a feel judgment then…I just give the pure yardage and say it's a little bit uphill or a little bit downwind….I caddy more by feel….I'm more of a feel person….I think a good caddy that has been with his player long enough would know what sort of shot their player's going to play. I mean that's part of being a good caddy: you don't have to ask your player about a certain shot. There are times when you see a different opinion on a shot, but most of the times you know what sort of shot they're going to play. You know how he plays his wedges; you know what he likes to do, and what he doesn't like to do. You don't have to ask, its just instinct. There are some situations that you come across where [there] might be two or three different ways to play a shot. You ask a player 'What do you see?' 'What sort of shot do you have

*in your head?' You tell them how far it is and what you
see.*

Summary

Steve processes the information and has an idea about the
shot as he approaches the ball. He tells his players the
yardage and the club he thinks it is straight away, so that they
have something to work from. If the yardage is affected by
wind or slope he will add this as a feel statement and the
suggested club to go with it. Steve believes after working with
a player you get to know exactly how he would intend to play
the shot anyway and thinks that you are unlikely to be too far
off what the player is thinking.

Saying the Right Things at the Right Time Involves Understanding What the Message is and the Best Way to Convey it

A: *I think when you are a caddy, you've got to work to think of
the right thing to say at the right time and that's…fairly
important: to be able to know when to say something
[and] when not to say something….It's just something you
learn [with] each player: when to speak to and when not
to speak to them; and…it's something you've got to learn.
It's something you've got to realise when you form a
relationship with a player, when he likes to be spoken to
or doesn't like to be spoken to, and when he needs
something positive said….If you want to have a
relationship, that's one of those things you work out with a
player, coz when the time comes [you] know when to say
something: what he likes to hear and then what he
doesn't like to hear.*
Q: How do you assess that?
A: *It's just second nature. I mean it's not something you
assess, it's just [that you] know when the situation calls, if
something needs to be said or doesn't need to be said. It
becomes natural, like when you're working with a player
on a regular basis, it just becomes part of it. You know*

when to say something and when not to say something.....When you talk with them, players are very predictable; surely y'know, when you get into a situation, or something, it's obvious you don't want to say the same things every time because...it's a bit like a broken record....You always like to say something different, but kind of get it across the same way. But not always say the same thing, so your player actually hears the message...you're trying to convey the same message, [but] you're always getting it across in different ways.

Dealing with specific situations such as poor play:

A: Sometimes when you start out the day and...things...are not going so good, and yeah, you gotta maybe talk about how you can influence your stroke play: 'let's just make it our goal to get to this number today' or 'not make any more mistakes'; what[ever] it might be....If things go badly...you've got to point out that there's so many holes to go and you can knuckle down and make X amount of birdies or get those shots back, or 'hey you've just got to forget that situation you were unlucky' or 'y'know, we made a mistake' or 'that was a bad break, we've got to get over it, we've got...how many holes left in the tournament?, we're still not out of it' or what ever it might be...you gotta [say]...whatever you think is the best thing to say at the time, but...it helps if the player...gets whatever message you're trying to get across...it depends on what you're saying, like if it's different to back then fine, otherwise if it's the same as back then you wouldn't hear it in the end.

To say everything thing confidently is crucial:

A: A good caddy is just someone who is very confident in what they do...someone that's done their homework, they're very confident and they're just confident in their ability as a caddy. I mean, no hesitation, not to be afraid of what you think. You're not always going to be right, but I think, as a caddy, providing you understand the way he plays, getting a feeling for when he's down or when he's up, when he's not confident, when he's confident, when he's pumped up or he's not pumped up take all those things into consideration...It's easier to not to have any doubt in your mind…you're not always going to be right, but if you always speak with a tone of voice that suggests that you have no doubt in your mind.

Summary

Knowing when to say what has come with experience for Steve. It's also a matter of phrasing perhaps the same or similar messages differently so that the player will hear them. Talking about things that will motivate your player when things aren't going well are perfect examples. But above all whatever you say needs to be given to the player confidently.

Debriefing on the Round Afterwards

A: After a round…you actually…sorta summarise how the day went, [where] you did particularly well, good area, or you had trouble with this hole, whether we can work it out…when you go to practice tee afterwards. A lot of times you go to the practice tee and you've played well, you just go to the tee to wind down, some days you go to the practice tee to work on things. You might…tell the player…what you saw…that you perhaps think you saw earlier on that he was doing wrong today, how he was swinging it….Or just say 'we had a bit of trouble on this hole' or 'we struggled on this hole, perhaps we should play it this way tomorrow' or…things like that.

Q: Do you ever discuss the effectiveness of your relationship with your players?

A: No.

Q: Can I ask why?

A: I don't think that's necessary…the results speak for themselves, if you're good…if you're having a good relationship, well it'll affect it; if you're not having a good relationship, it'll affect that…so I think that'll speak for itself.

102

Summary

Steve likes to regularly talk to his players after a round about what worked and what they could do better the next day. In terms of the success of the relationship, he thinks the proof is in the pudding. What you put in is what you'll get out of it.

The Player and Their Goals

A: *Every player...normally wants to win the tournament; [it's] the ultimate goal to start with, there's no question about that....If you're not there to try to win, you shouldn't be in the field. Of course as the tournament progresses, those goals may change. Sometimes you...realise you may not be able to win the tournament or you may not be able to make the cut. Your goal becomes to...just to do the best you can to make the cut, or if you barely make the cut...you've struggled; your goal might be to finish in the top twenty or the top ten. At the start of the week, everyone should have the same goal: trying to win the tournament. As the week goes on, your goals might change.*

Q: Would they, [your players] set score goals or...?

A: *Nah...you can't really set [them]. I mean a lot of weeks you have a general idea what...the score's gonna be. The weather plays such a big factor and the course conditions...but at the start of the week you have...a general idea what the weather's gonna be like for the week, and what the course is gonna play; you have a general idea but...you can't go out and say 'I'm going to shoot this score,' you always try and shoot the best possible that you can on the day, not a particular score....Golf takes so much concentration; I mean, once you're out at the golf course, then you need to concentrate and visualise the picture of your shot; there's not enough time [for score goals, like hitting a certain number of fairways]; they're too distracting. I mean once you're out there, try and shoot the best score you can on that day.*

Q: Long-term goals are okay though?

A: At the start of the season, you might have a goal, say you want to lower your putting average, or you need to hit more fairways or more greens; those are the goals you set at the start of the year...and you work your way through...but not on a week to week basis....[With my player] I'll have a fair idea of what we're working on [and] what we're trying to get to [goal-wise].

Q: If you know what [the goals] are, whether that's indirectly or directly, does that affect the way that you operate as a caddy?

A: No, a hundred percent not! I mean, I do the same job, day in and day out...like you know you want to do X; you set certain goals and that, but that doesn't...affect the way that you operate; you are always going to do the same things, whether winning or making the cut.

Summary

Setting goals is important for the player, and to Steve the ultimate goal that a professional golfer should be setting is to win. Setting specific score goals are not particularly helpful, in Steve's mind, but having an idea as to what sort of score will win, given the conditions on the day, is important for the success of the caddy-player team and the game plan chosen for the day. However, a player's personal goals do not affect the way Steve operates as a caddy.

Case Study 2: MARK FULCHER

Players he has worked with on the LET, LPGA, and men's European Tour include Gordon Brown Senior, Jamie Spence, Laura Davies, Alison Nicholas, Paula Marti, Sophie Gustafson, and Suzann Pettersen.

Please note: Due to a recorder malfunction, some of the paragraphs below do not represent direct quotes; they are, however, notes written during the interview and have been approved by Mark. These notes are identified by the use of "N."

The Attraction of Caddying

N: I first started caddying in 1978 at the age of 13 years in Cornwall, U.K., where I caddied for Gordon Brown, Sr. I also played golf and thus got interested. But because I wasn't as good a player, I decided to go for caddying. Here I get the opportunity to stand next to a good player—something that is unique to golf—you can't do it in football, for example. You can't go out on the field and help someone take a penalty, for instance, but you can in golf.

N: At the time of the interview I'd been caddying for 18 years on the ladies' tours and 2-3 years on the men's tours. I started my professional caddying career in 1984.

How Did He Come About His Job at the Time of Interview?

N: I worked the Evian Masters for this player. An opportunity opened for me, as she phoned me up and asked if I could work with her. As I thought I could help her, I said yes.

Mark explained that:

N. This caddy job came about because I've been out there; I know the players.

Preparation/Expectation of the Player and Setting Standards

Mark believes that doing the basics is important:

N: She is fussy and expects a lot. Yes, it's easy because I've always worked for fussy players. The expectation is always there. As soon as you do it once, she expects it from then on. The preparation of making your player feel as comfortable as possible is important. If she is comfortable she'll feel special. You kind of set the standard for yourself.

A: I have every bit of information written down in the book...so it can be (click, click of the fingers) like that....If I'm phaffing about saying 'yeah it's ah fifty-eight to the back and ah ten over the bunker it'll irritate her....Every now and then I will do that; I'm not quite prepared, and it will irritate her...but I would say ninety-five percent of the time it's there, I know what she wants. I am at an advantage; I know what she wants and she'll get it....Sometimes you have to accept that, if you don't do some [yardages correctly]. As long as they [the players] put everything into perspective, and if you do have a chat and say 'look it was a mistake,' you gotta put everything into perspective.

Q: You usually do more than most caddies?

A: When you set high standards, the trouble is they find out pretty swiftly [that] you don't always get that.

Q: If you had the chance to train a caddy, what skills would you suggest that he would need to acquire?

A: Basics. Get all the basics right....Be on time, clean the clubs, put up the yardage, walk the course, get as much information as you can....Just do all the basics and look after your player....Sometimes you dig your own grave. The more you do, the more they expect.

Summary

Being prepared, by doing all the basics well, walking the course, and gaining as much information as possible, helps Mark set his standards high as a caddy. High standards also means that his players come to expect it all the time, and this means that if he fails to do something quick enough or accurately enough it can annoy his players.

Friendship Qualities: A Difference between Men and Women

Keeping the Faith

N: *Having "faith" in your player is very important...as this comes across to your player.*
Q: Has your player developed trust in you?
N: *Yes. She trusts my basic yardages because I am ninety-nine point nine percent right. She asks for advice on club selection and for swing advice, so she must trust me. And she tells me things only I should know as well.*
A: *When we're out there, I think we both try and be professional and try and break it up in between [shots] with...light-hearted conversation....When you have an element of trust, when you've been with somebody for a while, like friends, you can talk about things that, I don't mean personal things, but I mean you can have opinions which you know aren't going to go out...that are special to you and [her]....You need to do your job, obviously, as we talked about, but...your responsibilities are your friendships, and to them as your friend and your boss; you've got to be loyal I think. Obviously, sometimes when caddies show loyalty and they get the sack then...things turn quite sour....And I think generally it works when caddies show loyalty to the player but...I think loyalty...to the cause, when things are going well, it's easy. We won the last two tournaments; life's good. Miss five out of six tournaments each summer, it would be very easy for both of us to think 'it's not working out'....Its one thing that gives me confidence, because...we've had this [win], it's happened twice to us now. Missed five cuts last [few tournaments] on the trot...mid season slump, and obviously struggled, and I never felt that she's at any point put any pressure on me. She's made me feel useful to her, and I'm very grateful for that. I keep plugging away*

at what we're trying to do....We [as caddies] have to put things in perspective...and I try to do that....I mean...with...[my player], I see a long-term future and we've got goals...and as I say...[she] never gives me anything; she never actually says to me 'y'know your doing fantastic'; she never says to me 'your doing shit'; so its very difficult to read [her]....I wouldn't know if she was happy or not happy...half the time.

Summary

To have mutual trust with his player is important to Mark. One of the best indicators that his player trusts him is that she relies on his yardages and clubbing advice. But above all, there is an ability to share personal thoughts and observations with each other, that they both know won't leave their caddy-player team unit. In return, Mark shows loyalty to his player by sticking by her and believing in her even if things are not easy, or even if there is little feedback. Having faith in the success of their relationship into the future is also part of the loyalty that Mark gives his players.

Balancing the Work and Pleasure Aspects of the Caddy-Player Relationship

Mark has both a friendship and a working relationship with his player. Whilst they are friends, this doesn't affect their working relationship. Between the player and caddy there needs to be a:

N: Personality match. You need to be able to relate to different players. Women are different to men, they want friendship and loyalty. Men just want you to do the work and leave. I used to caddy for Jamie Spence and that was the case; LET players involve you in their life more than the men. Yes, as a caddy, you can get too close to a player. For example, one caddy and his player, they got too close because they are good friends. It's getting that fine balance between business and pleasure. It's important to be all business on course. For example, two of my old bosses, Laura (Davies) and Ali (Nicholas) are

108

my best friends. Some players like to go out and eat with you because they are your friend and not just your boss. However, you can be a good caddy without being a friend. You don't spend time being their friend; it's just inevitable that you become friends, if your caddy-player relationship lasts.

Summary

Inevitably, you tend to become friends with your players (women usually want this), and your loyalty is part of a long-term caddy relationship package. However, it is a fine balance to keep as you can get too close. With men, they more often want just a working relationship with you; that's just fine with Mark, as he can still be a good caddy without needing to be the player's friend.

Being the On-course Sport Psychologist Involves Both Personality Assessment and Body Language

Mark believes that he motivates his players:

N: *I have to play sport psych out on the course. For example, at one tournament I wrote Thomas Bjorn on the yardage book, waited a little bit, after her reaction, her poor starting hole, and then said to her 'have a look at this.' She said 'What's that about?' 'Well, he had an eight at the British Open and then he went on to lead it. Come on, you can do it too!'*

Mark helps his players stay in the moment:

N: *After a penalty shot once, I said 'Don't think of the result, think of the action. Like a penalty shot for the FA cup, it's ACTION only. Not the result; you just do it.'*

A: *Every player's different...there are some you need to talk to more than others...but generally [my past players], they've all been relatively similar when they've all been friends.*

Q: How do you know if you need to talk to one more than the other?

A: *I think it's just different ways that's all. With [one player she] used to...moan a little bit and you used to have to try*

109

make her positive. [With another player] you just have to make her laugh. There's just all sorts...just...try and suit it to their personality and what you think they need....I think it's really nice sometimes when you have a relationship where, like when I worked for [one player]...it's an absolute all team, an all on-team effort....I feel me and [my current player] are getting closer to that. But [she's] a different person....[One of my old players] could be a fun time...'Come on mate, let's make this birdie, let's finish it'....[My current player is] used to go[ing] down...the back in peace, so [I] just [say] quiet things...just quietly... just different things for different players.

Assessing his players involves:

A: Body language. You know when she fancies a hole and when she doesn't fancy a hole...it's the body language and the way she [is] being, the way she talks about the hole. Perhaps when she's on the tee, she'll stand there, and she's, instead [of] taking the driver...she might be thinking what to do. I think it's a judge of character...sometimes you get it right, sometimes you don't. But generally...you can ask her a question. If she stands there and then takes the driver out, you say 'well, you too thinking of taking three wood out?' or something like that...and I'll walk up to the tee. It happened in the last couple of weeks. I'm thinking three wood off this tee; it's not driver, like we did yesterday, and as we walk off the green, I can almost sense that she might be thinking the same, so I say...to her, 'you thinking what I'm thinking?' and if she says 'no,' I think 'well she's not.' She might say 'what?' I know, but chances are she'll say 'yeah I am. Three wood yeah?'

Summary

As a caddy, Mark is essentially his player's on-course sport psychologist; he motivates and keeps her mind firmly on the task at hand. It also involves his ability to assess and adapt to the different needs of the player he is working with, and being able to read his player's body language so he can respond as effectively as possible to every individual situation that his player is in.

Effectiveness of the Player–Caddy Relationship: The Role of Feedback

N: *I believe that my current player rarely gives me any credit, but she does say thanks. She says things, but I'm not sure if we are working or not, simply because I am not getting the feedback. I can only assume we are working well because of the changes I've observed in her attitude and performance.*

Q: Do you discuss the effectiveness of your relationship with your players?

A: *Sometimes. [My player] always says to me, whether we shoot eighty-five or sixty-five, 'Well done, great job.' Very rarely [she] says to me 'there you really didn't make the grade' – that's just the way [she] is… But I think we do, yes we do; like yesterday, go to the range and have dinner and [she] will mention it discretely: 'There were four bad clubs out there yesterday.' We talk, just little bits…about it, [she'll] just mention it to me, and then…I'll say 'we need to…work on it a little bit, adjust it a little bit better.'*

Q: Are you helping her?

A: *Yes, I think so.*

Summary

Mark and his player discuss their team's on-course performance from day to day, but never really discuss the true effectiveness of their relationship. Beyond thanking him, his player doesn't give any specific verbal feedback to Mark, so he can only extrapolate from her attitude and behaviour as to his general success.

The Gelling of a Player and Caddy is Often Dependant on the Length of Time Together

A: *I think that's experience; knowing each other.*

Q: The more time you're working with each other?

A: *Yeah, definitely invaluable. It just seems to me now days a lot of players and caddies don't stay together long enough. There seems to be lots of changes going on at the moment.*

Q: Do you think it's good to have a long-term relationship with a caddy?

A: *I was with Ali [Nicholas] four years, was with Laura [Davies] quite a while. I think it is good but…sometimes I think you need to freshen it up; it can get dull, coz [it could] end up stale, but I think it's good [to work together long-term]. You can get two who really fit well; [with a] bit [of] security there, you can work much better….I think it would be fantastic if you find the right gel. For a player, it needs to be right. And there're so many different varieties of characters out there; there're so many different caddies….I think [my current player's] happy with they way I work with her. But if…for the first few months it didn't work out, then there is no doubt about it [you'd finish the relationship]. If you feel uncomfortable out there with your caddy you're in trouble because he's there all the time, or she's there…and that's no good.*

N: *It's very much a liquid job. You can be fired for anything: being late, bad, or simply because the player wants a change.*

Summary

Mark believes that it is important to have the right caddy-player gel. An opportunity to build a really good relationship requires a caddy and player to work together for a significant period of time—although you would know if the gel was wrong within the first few months.

The Caddy Keeping the Player Confident and Committed

Q: How important is it for you to make sure your player is confident?

A: *Essential. I'd say to her, even if I disagree with a club, and I have done…I'd always agree with her in the end. I would*

112

say 'that's a good club, I agree with you'….I'll say my opinion, and if she doesn't take my opinion, then what the hell, there's no point taking sides….You're always better off hitting a good shot with a bad club, than a bad shot with a good club….Better to be over the back and hit it well…coz then you['ve] got a reason why you did it. But if you hit a bad shot you never know. I always believe it's best to hit a good shot than a bad one….You can't ever commit and put your best swing on it, if you're not sure about the club.

Q: How do you go about making sure your player's a hundred percent committed and confident?

A: *By the time it comes to the decision, you both agree and you're like 'right let's produce a shot here'….Nine times out of ten she doesn't need it, but every now and again; like seventeen yesterday, we disagreed on a club and she took seven iron out, and just as she was in preparation, I say to her 'perfect club that, that's spot on'….Maybe it makes her feel better, maybe it doesn't, but…when she stands over the club… she thinks 'right.' As it turns out, she hit a beauty. One bounce and [it was] over the back of the green.*

Q: How about with her confidence on the long-term versus short-term basis?

A: *[If] we start the season okay, and then we have a bad run, I will try and say 'y'know, we can work on things,' 'the short game, you gotta start believin' in it' and 'we gotta work a little bit harder and it'll come through,' and…this year it has…it's paid off, but yes, I think it is part of, especially a long-term caddy's job, to stay with them, remind them of the positives, remind them of what their working on and that golf…isn't [just] about one shot or the next shot or the next round or the next tournament; its about the long term thing….I keep plugging away at what we're trying to do.*

Q: Do you think that [loyalty] feeds off both of you?

A: *Oh yeah, definitely.*

113

Summary

Creating confidence in his player at shot level is crucial to Mark, and he does this by affirming his player's choice of club so she can fully commit to it. Mark would like to see his players be fully committed on every shot. On a long-term basis, Mark will remind his player of the overall picture, will offer encouragement, and will remain loyal.

Staying Emotionally Balanced as a Caddy

Q: Do you see it as part of your role to increase her confidence?

A: *Yeah, I think if she's down, if she's having a bad day, yeah, absolutely; that's my [job]. I help to do everything I can to make her perform her best. If the caddy's head goes down, [the] players notice it very quickly....And I try, specifically; if she's hit a bad shot...to have a neutral reaction...it's very important, [as] they look at you....If we miss the cut she's very, very disappointed, but I've got to show her...I'm disappointed....There's two ways you gotta...be, not like I'm taking it personally myself...but then other times you've got to....She hits a shot and doesn't get the bounce, I'll get angry cause I am angry...you've got to show that you care as well. So, there's a difficult line there.*

Q: Okay, so how do you know that line?

A: *I don't know...I just try my best.*

Summary

Mark thinks it is crucial to keep his head up and be neutral in his reactions when his player is down. At the same time, he likes the player to know that he cares and this can be a fine line to balance.

Conversations: Knowing When to Say What

A: *I think if you can figure out their personalities...you can figure out what's best to say and what's not to say. Often it's the case of not to say anything is better.*

Q: So if in doubt say nothing?

A: *Oh yeah, definitely.*

Q: How do you know when to say what?

A: *I know she's a bit quick. I know how she swings the club and the mistakes she makes that...produce bad shots. So if I pre-empt something, I think this is going through her mind, that's left or something and it's right and she backs away and you can tell her 'just nice and smooth.' Just little pointers that if I think something might be coming to her mind, as in a bunker, or where she shouldn't hit it, I try and get her mind focused on something good....I think I am quite good at pre-empting that. And if she's hit a bad shot, and then the next shot always, she'll ask me 'what have I done?'....[I'll] say 'that was a bit quick on the takeaway' or 'you didn't finish your back swing' or 'your hips were a bit quick.' Something just to reassure her really that that was a bad shot but there's no need to think it's going to continue.*

Q: When you're talking about pre-empting, what cues, or what things do you pick up on?

A: *Well I think it's body language.*

Summary

Saying the right things at the right time is all about understanding your player's personality for Mark. It's about reading her body language and taking a risk and saying something when you think it is most appropriate to do so.

Talking in Between Shots

A: *It always makes me laugh; the first thing any player [and] caddy...always talks about [is] 'What'd you do for dinner last night?'....It's a standard line, which always makes me laugh because...it means basically that you've got nothing to say, so it's a classic line to begin [with]....I think the better you know your player the less...small talk there is....You get on with business, and then you find [as] the course of the day goes on, you just...talk about stuff... but you don't have to force it. When you're with a new player...you have to find things to talk about because obviously you don't know enough about them, you don't know what they want to talk about and stuff.*

Q: What period of time do you tend to move from small talk into getting to know a player?

A: Six months.

Team Work: Talking About Shot Choice

A: [My] routine is basically, I'll go up and get the yardage....I'll tell her the yardage straight off the top of my head....She wants to know...front, pin, back, and where the wind direction is, all the basics....And then she'll ask me the question. I'm of the caddying opinion that caddies should never tell a player what club it is....They should advise and...if she said 'seven,' instead of saying 'no I don't I think [so], it's six'....I always give a reason: 'well don't you think the wind's slightly into, perhaps...?' [or] 'Are you considering...?' And to be honest, I s'pose it's a bit of a cowardly way, but it's a way of making them think they make the decision.

Q: So that they own it?

A: Yeah, I think so, because there is nothing worse as a player being told...I've done that in the past....Very few players, but some players...like that....If you sometimes say 'seven, is this good?' Then the answer's got to be positive, not 'maybe,' 'could be.' 'Perfect club,' y'know. That's different. But when you're trying to change their mind, I always try and give them reasons why they should change their mind... Then they can think about it and if [my player] agrees she will, if she doesn't she won't....With [my player] the final decision is hers, it always has been. Rarely do I say 'absolutely not.'

Q: How much do you actually convey to your player?

A: Just the standards all the time. Front yardage, flag yardage, always the back edge with...her. Wind direction is essential, and they're standard. And then she'll come back with the question 'what do you think it's playing?'...'Do you think six is enough?' Y'know 'How far's that over that bunker?'

Empowering the Boss in the Process

A: As I've matured as a caddy, I think the less bossy I've become...so I don't feel like I have to justify myself. I think the less experienced caddies feel they have to justify themselves, like 'well I change[d] the club there' and 'I told her the line here' and 'it was the wrong club like I said'....It's justification, and there should not be any justification from either side, it should be just trying to get the best of the job I think....We're not trying to score points against each other; we're trying to ensure we've got the right club....We ask questions of each other...'What's the wind doing?' 'What do you think its playing? Y'know, 'what sort of shot should we hit?'....I'll stand there...and if I can sense a problem, then I'll say 'well perhaps we can try this, perhaps we can try that'...but never ever tell them what to do....Number one [rule] for caddies: Don't tell your player what to do; it only lead[s] to trouble....I'm no swing coach, but I can see one or two things that she does which create bad shots and I point them out but that's all. [It's] all said quietly...you can't be 'oh [so and so] that was...' Just a little tap, let her walk down the fairway, say 'just a little advice there...' and walk away and that's it... it goes in, she won't say thanks or whatever, it just gives her something to focus on. She's very much, it's her game. One of her ex-caddies... said to her 'I made you'...he caddied for her and took her to the next level, was with her, and I think, he kept saying to her, 'y'know, you'll be nothing without me'. I certainly think that's had an effect, coz now she does everything herself....I think she thinks I'm good for her, but I think...in her head...she needs to do it for herself.

Q: And do you think that's important from a caddy's perspective?

A: *I think it's really nice sometimes when you have a relationship where...it's an absolute all team—an all on team effort....I feel me and [my current player] are getting closer to that. But [she's] a different person...and I think...she's got too much to carry round.*

Summary

Mark believes in letting his players make the club choice themselves—or at least allowing them to think that they do. Choosing a club and shot is a team effort where he, as the caddy, provides the basic information such as the yardage, and then he let's the player ask questions and choose a club from there. He doesn't feel the need to have to tell his players what to do, as he sees more value in them arriving at the decision themselves.

His Player's Goals and Determination

A: *I know what her rough goals are. So [in] saying we don't [set goals], the last few weeks we have - so far so good....We both know we need to step it up this week.*

Q: Does it affect the way you operate, if you know her rough goals?

A: *Well I think it makes...you more determined doesn't it? Possibly, this aim has made her more determined.*

Q: Do you ever make a game plan together?

A: *We always have a game plan, how we are going to play the course, yeah. What clubs we give ourselves, and sometimes it changes...if we have a practice round [My player] always plays an eighteen hole practice round [and] we try and work out exactly together...what we think and...what angles we're going to come in from and how she should play the hole and if she misses the green she misses it here....I think we have long term plans....I think...both of us would like us to become top five player in the world. And...even though she's not, as hands on as like working with [other players]....I think she thinks the*

same to a point. She thinks that we're a team and…we're
going to achieve those goals sometime in the future.

Summary

Mark roughly knows his player's long-term goals and he
thinks this helps both him and his player be more determined.
Week-to-week goals of game-plan setting is done together.
He thinks his player considers them to be a team with a
future.

Case Study 3: FRED "BASSETT"

Players he has worked with on the LET include Debbie Dowling, Gillian Stewart, Jane Connachan, Dale Reid, Corrine Dibnah, Sandrine Mendiburu, Judith Van Hagen, Karen Lunn, Gwladys Nocera, and Cecilia Ekelundh.

Experience: How Fred Got Into Caddying

Q: How long have you been a caddy?

A: *Twenty-two years… I've been on European Men's Tour…and the Seniors Tour…and on the Ladies [Tour].*

Q: And is it fun work?

A: *Oh great, yeah…great…The only thing that isn't fun is the travelling…in between tournaments; but once you're there…*

Q: Is it then that the fun kicks in?

A: *Yeah. I caddied as a child for pocket money…and then when I left school I got a job and I played golf…Then I was made redundant and I just drifted into it. There was an event down at me local golf course. I went down there and caddied for a guy…it was a PGA event, like [the] club pro's…championships. And he asked me to go to the next one, and…I did that, and I did a few more with him that year. And the year after, them ladies came to the same course…and I got a job there and then. I started on the Ladies [Tour]… and that sort of snowballed….[I had] no intention of doing it as a job….[I] took one [job] then another one then another….And obviously, once you get yourself known, people start to make you offers, [then] you can afford to do it as a living….To start with…you're the bottom of the ladder and…it doesn't pay that much….It's like any job really, you start at the bottom of the ladder and if you're any good you'll go up it. If you're no good, you won't.*

Beginnings and Endings with Players Keeps You on Your Toes

Q: How long have you been working with [your current player]?

A: Two years.

Q: How did your caddy-player relationship come about?

A: I've known her for years...for a long while, and obviously [me] being on the Tour and she needed a caddy...she approached me.

Q: Did you do any research of your player prior to...taking on her bag?

A: No, [coz] I'd known her, I'd seen her play....I've worked a lot for [one particular player] over the years, on and off...we're very good friends...off the golf course as well....She's a bit fiery...so sometimes, she fires me...but we're still the best of mates...it's just one of those things....Y'know, what [she] is like...hard work sometimes, but we're still the best of mates.

Q: How did your working relationship come to an end with [your previous player]?

A: It was the end of the year and she just didn't ask me for the year after [and] I didn't ask her....I didn't mind....If they don't want me they don't want me, there's always someone else...so it's just the way it is. They say change is as good as a rest anyway, sometimes...it's very unusual for a player-caddy relationship to last and last and last, it doesn't happen very often....Working for one person all the time, you get to know everything you do; it's like you get blasé more-a-less...you coast through...it's so easy....But when you're out with someone who['s] sorta relying on you maybe a bit more...it keeps you on your toes, it gets you thinking...and it freshens things up a bit, it keeps your interest a bit more lively....If you work for one player you get a bit blasé...but if you go working for another player they won't, they have different needs to your player....Like I say, I've been here twenty-odd years; I know most of the girls I've caddied for, loads of them...so I know the different personalities.

Summary

Fred's long term presence on the Tour means he's been able to work for the same players on and off and to know his players before he takes them on. When they do come to an end, he keeps it amicable. He is never too concerned, as there is always work around the corner. Continually working for lots of different players helps keep you on your toes. It helps you avoid getting blasé. Working for other players helps Fred keep sharp when it comes to reading personalities too!

Attraction to LET Versus the Men's European Tour

A: I've taken years off, a couple of years here and there, but [worked] mainly on the Ladies [Tour].

Q: Why, is it the best tour?

A: For me it is…because they're a…friendlier crowd for a start. They're all friendly….The money's not massive…so there isn't that much pressure….You're not continually on the road….I've had clubs thrown at me, balls thrown at me and not on the Ladies Tour, I might add….Yes, the Men's Tour is full of bitches; there's more bitches on the Men's Tour than on the Ladies, believe me. I've been hit with golf clubs, I've been hit in the eye with a golf ball…and that you do NOT take…some do, I don't, I've walked off the course….I've self-respect.

Helping out Young Players

A: [There] are the people I caddy for but I also help out one or two young girls.

Q: Like [one young girl]; she likes picking your brains?

A: Yeah, coz she's a bit fiery…and I think she's too quick….She's the sort of player who's got talent but because she can't afford a caddy she's on her own all the time. [It only] takes two bad shots and she needs somebody…[or she'll be] throwing the towel in…so I like working for people like that….I don't get paid for it; I just do it for the fun of it….When [a more established player] started out [she] was the same; she was skint…and I used to go out and help her out, like I'd finished my eighteen holes and I'd go out and do another nine with [her].

Q: Does [your current player] mind you going out and helping the others?

A: *No not at all, some would [she] doesn't….Actually, I don't do it in tournaments now….I shot myself in the foot one year; we lost; [this now established player] won by one shot and I'd done two days with her…so I'd helped her out; so I'd shot myself in the foot a little bit so…I don't do it in tournaments. In my spare time, I'll do it on practice days.*

Q: Do you get your player's permission to help others?

A: *Oh yeah, you must do….I…wouldn't dream of doing it without permission; no way; that sort of thing's just not on….Some players…would not let you do it…but [my player] doesn't mind, she knows I'm doing it as a favour…and it's no real threat to her.*

When working with younger players Fred will:

A: *Talk a lot more to [them] than I do to [my proper player]….I have more to do….She might question [my facts] more than [my proper player]…and she might ask my opinion about what kind of shots [to play].*

Summary

Fred has gained a lot of experience over his long career as a tour caddy working for a variety of different players. He prefers working on the LET as he finds them friendlier than the Men's Tour, where he has felt he has been mistreated in the past. His work on the Ladies Tour is a labour of love, as he likes to help young players who can't afford to pay for a caddy.

Trust and Effective Relationships: Player Trusting Caddy

A: *She trusts me…but that trust takes time….You don't get that instantly [the] first time.*

Q: How does that come about?

A: She probably checks decisions; if it's on the fence, and I disagree with her, I think she has the final decision...and as I say, if you're any good...they learn to trust you and it's a good working relationship.

Q: Has [she] developed trust in you now?

A: Yeah...I'd say at least ninety percent, yes. [What] I like about her, [and] like about working for [her] is if we disagree about a club and I'm right, and she's wrong, she will tell me...she'll say 'Oh sorry Fred'...she'll apologise to me....and...there's no conflict. The fact that we disagree doesn't create a conflict.

Q: When did the trust develop in your relationship?

A: About a couple of weeks...let us say...after about six rounds....[I knew because]...she asked questions, basically....Obviously, I do the yardage...so she knows that's always right, and she'll ask me if she's between clubs, [although] she pulls the club herself....I give her the yardage, and she pulls the club. But if there's any sort of doubt in her mind, she'll ask me what my opinion is, and then obviously the final decision is hers. I don't get many wrong, but everybody gets them wrong...sometimes. Nobody's perfect....I don't look upon it as a mistake; it's an error of judgment.

Fred knew she trusted him because she started to ask for his opinion.

Q: What factors, as a whole, do you think build trust in a caddy-player relationship?

A: Foremost, I think punctuality....[When] they get here in the morning, your there. They don't want to be looking around for you wondering whether you're going to turn up or if you're late....So I think punctuality is the main thing. You gotta be here...and then [you] don't want to turn up at the course without a wash and a shave in the morning....But I'm...old school...you get some of the younger lads who couldn't give a damn. But that's a personal thing....I'm not saying that does make them any worse as a caddy, but it's just that I'm a bit of an old fart, I s'pose....Keep yourself clean and tidy and don't go drinking at the golf course...to excess anyway! Just behave yourself generally, and if you wish to misbehave, do it away from the golf and the golf course....Here you wouldn't dream of that...it's free beer here this week, but I wouldn't stay here getting plastered... just have a couple, but...we've had lads in the past who [got] just absolutely plastered...just because it's free...and then they make an exhibition of themselves....It's not on!

Q: Coz the rules are that the players get fined if their caddies misbehave?

A: *Yeah that's true...the player is responsible for the caddy's behaviour.*

Q: How long did it take you to build trust with [your past player]?

A: *Well I'd caddied for her when she first came over from [abroad] which'd be fifteen or sixteen years ago...so...that year it didn't take long to remember the way she worked; it took one round to adjust...coz she knows me from years ago.*

Summary

It's important to Fred to have his player's trust him, and he knows he's gained this trust when she starts asking for his opinion. Being reliable and taking pride in your appearance and behaviour also help build trust between player and caddy. The time this trust takes can vary depending on how well he knows the player and if he has worked with the player before.

Friendship Versus Business

A: *You know some[times]...you can work with somebody, you've been the best of friends off the golf course, but on a golf course it just doesn't work out, sometimes....Sometimes you can be too friendly...with them.*

Q: Tough judgement call?

A: *Yes, you just gotta learn....I've been sacked many a time...not because I just wasn't doing the job. You just can be too close...or just not gelling....I think you have to like each other....You don't have to be...bosom pals or*

125

anything…because sometimes that's a hindrance, if you're too close. [You just need] friendship and respect for one another….I'm not too close to [my current player], I mean, she's not a close friend, coz I don't see [her] at all [off] course; it's just business but…there's nothing wrong with that….Like [two other players] and people like that, I go out to dinner with them at night….I have me friends away from [her]….I think that's good as well, I don't want to be in her pocket…and she don't want me around twenty-four hours a day.

Summary

Fred believes it's possible to get too friendly with players and then it doesn't work on the golf course. You need to have your space from each other. As long as you are friendly and have respect for each other, that is the main thing.

CONVERSATIONS: Switching off and Having a Laugh Between Shots

Q: What makes a good player–caddy relationship, from your point of view?

A: *Sense of humour….You need to…well, in my opinion…you need to switch off a little between shots….You don't want to be walking up to the ball thinking about your next shot; you do that when you get there. So if you can do, have a little bit of…small talk; not too much. You sort of learn…by experience when to…have a bit of small talk…a bit of a switch off for a little minute. Sometimes you don't, sometimes you keep away….You sort of learn that…it's instinct that….Just small talk, generally gossip, she talks about. Being a shapely girl, she's…very fashion conscious and so she talks about people's dress and…so we have a bit of laugh about that…and she's very fond of telling me who's put weight on and who hasn't put weight on…and I wouldn't notice….She notices everything, being a woman….We have a bit of a laugh…we have quite a few laughs, actually; she's good for [that], and I think you need some sense of humour…most important to have a*

126

sense of humour…just to switch off for a couple of minutes and just relax; I think it does, anyway.

Q: What things do you talk to your player about during a round?

A: *Family…coz [she's] got family…young child. I've got young grand children so we talk about family and…things like that…just small talk really. Health, coz mine's not that good….Just small talk; football, she's a football fan…to an extent…and with her being a woman, general gossip.*

Q: Would you not do that with a guy?

A: *Not so much in men's golf…there doesn't seem to be much camaraderie, really.*

Q: Is that why you prefer [the] women's [Tour]; is that all part of it?

A: *Yeah, it's just more relaxed atmosphere; I think….I'm easy going. I'm very easy going, so I…create a happy atmosphere when we're out on the golf course, a few good laughs…but then…when it's time to, we switch off….Like I say, between shots we switch off, and then when we get up to the ball it's business again.*

Summary

Switching off between shots and talking, gossiping, and having a laugh is an important part of the game. Fred believes it helps create a relaxed atmosphere.

Positive Encouragement and Guidance

Q: What specific things do you say to your player during a round, for example?

A: *Mainly encouragement….Don't mention the trouble! Any trouble on the course, you point that out during your practice rounds…out of bounds left, water on the right. You don't stand up on the tee box during a tournament and say negatives, you['ve] done that in the practice rounds…so you don't, no negatives on the golf course, always positives…and little words to lift 'em or just little word[s] of encouragement.*

Q: What if things are going well? What do you say? Like she's strung a whole bunch of birdies together?

A: *Give her a little pat on the shoulder and say 'well done'...'well played'; you don't get any high-five nonsense, that's for yanks...none of that; I don't go over board...but I do say 'well done' if she hits a good shot....Like I said, [say] positives all the time...different things all the time...'keep it going' y'know...'yeah, come on, let's keep it going, yeah'.....Never get ahead of yourself, never say...like 'God, that's three now, you're coasting up'....You might say little things like...'good swing there' y'know, and sometimes...you can see little faults that have [been] developing...they've come in....I'm not a qualified coach, so I don't confess to be...but sometimes you can see little things creeping in...and...she might stand up, and got like a tricky shot to a small target, and...a lot of players tend to try and guide it in...push it in rather than hit it...so you can see that, so you...try and tell 'em y'know 'just get through the ball and hit it through, through to the target'; they're the little things you pick up over the years.*

Summary

Fred believes in only talking about positives to his player when in a tournament. This includes encouraging her when things are going well, guiding her if swing faults start to creep in, and keeping her in the present.

Reading Personalities and Knowing When to Say Things

Talking:

A: *Sometimes you don't, sometimes you keep away...you sort of learn that...it's instinct that....You can't [teach it]....I mean it....If you work for different players as well, actually that helps...If you work for one player, you get a bit blasé...but if you go working for another player, they won't; they have different needs to your player....Like I say, I've been here twenty-odd years; I know most of the girls; I've caddied for loads of them...so I know the different personalities. I know when to keep my mouth shut...but that's knowing people....A new caddy wouldn't necessarily know that and [would] sometimes talk too much.*

Q: Do you think its getting to know their personalities...that's key to...whether you do the small talk or not...and when to shut up?

A: Yup.

Q: What kind of personality would you say lots to between shots and what kind of personality would you NOT say lots to?

A: Bad tempers; be wary...very wary. Then again, experience. I know most of the girls out here; I know [what] all their temperaments are like....So I have to...just stay out of the firing line, basically...get me head bit off [otherwise]....You['re] just learning; you know sometimes, you get it wrong.

Q: How do you know when to say what?

A: Well you don't....Like I said earlier on, [it's due to] my experience, really [and knowing] your player; knowing when to say something; and you never get it right all the time...there's no quick way of doing it, but conversation helps obviously....If you're just going to walk round and trudge along ten yards behind with the bag, you're not going to learn much....You're not going to learn their personality or anything. You've got to be upside them and talk...but if they don't want that, then you'll soon know; they'll soon let you know without being rude....All girls are different; all people are different...you get different kinds of personalities...so...you know the ones that are fiery...you're a little bit wary of them....Just have to be aware of the many different personalities, especially with the woman...and you have to read their moods as well.

Q: What makes you able to read people?

A: Watch people, even if you're not with them, even if you're not working for them. [If] you're paired with them, you can watch, you can see people's [reactions]. Sometimes...you can see [their personalities], like I have [with the young player I help out]. I know that she's a better player but...she needs a caddy....Not only her, there's loads of girls out here who would benefit from having a caddy, but the financial side of it, it's just too difficult for them....Another thing about the Ladies Tour, maybe well, I'll mention it to you... they can be very moody, so you keep a low profile...I won't go into names, but I'm sure [you] can...y'know, well...sometimes you have to be....And [their periods], sometimes it affects the game as well...definitely affects their game with folks....I understand what's going on; y'know what I mean?

Q: Just their monthly hormonal issues?

A: *Yeah...it's a factor in the ladies game, definitely....I know, I've worked for a good few girls, some, some got really nasty. You keep your distance.*

Q: If you've got a good ability to learn and observe and watch...that's the only way you're going to learn how to read a player....Would that be a good summary?

A: *You must yeah, it's the best way coz you're doing it quietly without disturbing anyone.*

Summary

Knowing when to say what is all about getting to know your player's personality, according to Fred. This involves being aware of hormonal issues; especially if they are women, watching and observing players, even if you are not working with them; and talking with them.

Talking about Club Selection

Q: When you start talking business stuff do you...change the way you talk?

A: *Yeah, coz it's matter of fact; I give her facts and figures that's all....I make statements. [For example], I give her the yardage...I tell her the wind direction and how far the pins on the green [are] and just give her the information she needs to know....Then she might ask me, 'what did we have yesterday?'...so I give her yesterday's yardage, coz I write it all down everyday...so I give her yesterday's yardage and we compare the two. Obviously, I don't say [a] club unless she asks me; if she asks me what club, then I'll tell her. [I] say what I think…I just dish the facts and the figures and then she'll ask and I'll tell her what I think. I won't wait until she suggests…what she thinks. I tell her what I think, then what she's got in mind is….If it's not the same [as] what I had, it's up to her; she has to make a decision then…and sometimes she'll ask me, 'do you think it's…?' Based on…yardage, wind direction, and things; just based on facts that we got, black and white, here…and obviously, I know how far they hit it; I know the facts.*

Q: Do you tell her everything that you compute?

A: *Everything, as much as I can…yeah, but I don't tell her how to play the shot. I don't tell her whether to fade the shot…I don't tell her to hit it hard or soft….Obviously, you never get, well you don't 'never,' but a yardage that suits every club. Sometimes you get a yardage that's between clubs…then you might say 'well it's any easy eight' y'know or a 'hard nine'….That is for them to decide; whether they want to hit a soft eight or a big nine….That's not for me to decide….So I give them the front [and] yardage to the pin. But if there's X to carry over… one edge, maybe a bunker over the left side, I'll give 'em the extra carry…so I would tell her that's your carry and then the pin is…so the carry and the pin is only on five…so…actually it's on twenty and you've got fifteen extra carry on the left…and normally I'd just put a little pencil mark and say the pin's there…so she has…a picture of it as well…she can actually visualise it…as well as….Simple really; nothing hard about it….Sometimes she doesn't ask me which club…but I can see her thinking, and then I have a club in mind….I always…have an answer in mind…even if she doesn't ask me….I have my answer ready for her, so sometimes…she'll just pull (for arguments sake) a seven iron…and she'll select [it] for herself, and she pulls what I think's good, but I won't tell her. Sometimes I do, sometimes I will tell her 'I don't think that's enough.' I will put my neck on the line. [For example], in between distances…and if…I'm thinking it's a six and she pulls a seven, I might ([if] I know it's in between), I'll tell her 'you'll have to hit that'…'hit it,' 'just hit it'; 'yeah, a full seven' and I'll say things like that.*

Q: Are you ever uncertain about the choice?

A: *Yeah sometimes…you got to make your mind up sooner or later but…like I say, you get in between distances [and] she'll say, 'what do you think about the five iron?' I'll say, 'well yeah'….The biggest issue…because sometimes…the players, they'll take like a five iron, and you're between the five and the six, and you don't want to hit it [or] commit. You must commit. Once you pull that club, it's the right club…even if it turns out to be the wrong one. You must be positive and hit the ball; you must be positive with it. If it turns out to be the wrong one, you've made the wrong decision, but at least you've been positive. You know you can pull it and half hit it, that's negative….You must be positive. Once you've committed yourself to a club, it's the right club. If it turns out a bit awful, that's just too bad; you made a mistake….You must be positive….The number of times you see players sort of half hit shots, and make a mess of them, because they don't commit!*

Summary

Fred always has his information at hand and has a club in mind at all times. He believes in giving advice as a matter of fact, letting the player choose the club. However, he will say what he thinks without needing prompting and he will do this by backing the player's decision. Or, he will risk disagreeing (or suggesting) if it is between clubs (that it might need to be a full club). He wants his player to fully commit to the shot and be positive.

Caddy's Role: Responsibilities and Skills

Q: What are your responsibilities as a caddy?

A: *Always number[s], punctuality, reliability….If the weather's tough, [I've] gotta make sure we've got adequate clothing in the bag….Yep, just prepared for all weather conditions…everything really…extra towels, obviously [for] bad weather…as well as the clothing. Just make sure that you've got everything you might need. [On course], just do your job [and] make sure I get all the right yardages.*

Q: If you had the chance to train a caddy, what skills would you suggest that he would need to acquire?

A: *A sense of humour….I think that's very important, a smile on your face…punctuality again [is] first and foremost in my opinion….Appearance is very important…to me it is, and I think it should be to anyone, anyway…you should have pride in your appearance…in my opinion.*

Q: What makes a good caddy 'good'?

A: *Being able to get on with your player, being able to be at ease with your player, being able to feel that you can say and express your opinion [and work] together as a team….So you really have to have a mutual respect.*

Q: What is it that separates a top caddy from an average caddy?

A: *It's the player's opinion that counts.*

Q: What do players want from a top caddy?

A: *Reliability and knowing that…different players need different things. Like [my current player] doesn't need my help on the greens. I don't…do that. [It] is added pressure on the job…so…you have to be pretty confident on the greens….They soon find out who the good caddies are [and] who are not. Like the job offers you get really, [they want] somebody who they can get on with; [that] is…most important. You might not be the greatest caddy in the world…but if you're good company…out there…that is worth…a lot.*

Summary

Fred believes you need to be punctual, reliable, and tidy on course. He also believes that you need to be able to calculate yardages and be prepared for all weather. Most importantly, he suggests a good caddy needs to be able to get on with his player—this is where having a sense of humour helps.

Taking the Blame and Committing to a Call

A: *Some players will hit the shot and they'll blame you for everything....They'll never admit that they've made a mistake, but [my current player] does...which is better. It creates a better working relationship, because if you're gonna get blamed for everything...it puts you on edge...and you can sort of drift...to the attitude where you might sit on the fence a little bit...instead of committing yourself to what you think. Sort of sit on the fence, coz you don't want to commit yourself in case you get blamed for something that's not your fault.*

Q: Do you think it's important, as a good caddy, to commit yourself?

A: *Yeah, of course you do...you must be one hundred percent positive in your own ability. You know you would [be] found out if you weren't. [You] don't want to be a 'yes' man.*

Differences between his current and previous players:

A: *Much different...some blame (usually) the caddy but never to herself. The year I worked for her, she had a bad year but [my previous player] didn't [blame me]; she just had a bad year.*

When players blame Fred:

A: *If I consider it my fault, then I take it...it's part of the job...and sometimes I'll take it anyway when I know it's not my fault....I can tell when a player hits a ball fat or thin....I can tell when they hit it properly....Sometimes I take it; I know I didn't do it, but they're looking to blame you rather than themselves...I'll take so much of that, but...it just depends. [It's] better than some things, like having a row.*

If it is not Fred's fault he may say:

A: *I don't consider it 'my fault' whatever....You take a certain amount of abuse, it's part of the job....If they'd rather blame someone else than themselves, and it makes them feel better for it, all well and good; it's all part of the job. If it gets personal, really abusive, then you draw the line....I['ve] dropped the bag [before]....I dropped it on the hole, I'm not proud of what I've done; really I sort of…think I should of stuck it out, in hindsight…for a few holes…quit me job there and then, out on the golf course….You have to have a mind of your own…and speaking up now and again when you feel the time's right…you speak your mind…and sometimes they don't like it. Sometimes you have to be critical…you try and be constructive with your criticism…you're not trying to destroy their confidence or anything….What I've learnt over the years [is that] it's how you feel. Even though it might be critical, something needs to be said sometimes. Although sometimes…you need to say something to them and you get the sack….I put me neck on the line now and again if I feel I have to…if I feel it will benefit in the long run….Well sometimes it works, sometimes it doesn't, but…you've got to be confident enough…to do it. It's your job to do it.*

Summary

Fred feels that there is an element of risk involved when caddying. You need to commit to any decision or call you give to your player—you need to be confident in your ability as a caddy. This can be easier if the player is happy to blame herself as it givers him more confidence to take a stand in the decision-making process. However, sometimes it may involve taking the blame for poor performance, rightly or wrongly. And it may mean you need to say something to the player if it is going to help her overall performance.

Learning from Mistakes, Errors of Judgment, and Helping Keep the Relationship Effective

Q: What makes a good player-caddy relationship?
A: *Sense of humour.*
Q: Do you ever discuss the effectiveness of your relationship?
A: *No…I don't think you need to. No, I do my job, she does her job. We get on well together.*
Fred's current caddy-player relationship is effective because:
A: *The fact that we disagree doesn't create a conflict…*

Fred's philosophy:

A: *On the golf course, and [if] I['ve] made...an error of thinking, I should admit to my mistakes. [If there is a problem], she shoulda said [so] in the first place: to talk a little bit....I could've done [something about it].*

When Fred first takes on a player:

A: *Usually...if I'm working with somebody, I ask them 'do you like to talk between [shots]?' Some don't... I ask them if they want small talk. Basically I'm relaxed between [shots]...being myself...but some people don't, [they] prefer to be blinkered....I usually...tell them, if it's like the first tournament, if there's any anything that you want to say at the end of the week, say it...because...no offence is taken. I have to learn...what you want, coz if you don't tell me I won't know....I don't take it as criticism...I'd rather be told. And there's nothing worse than, if I'm doing something wrong, or the wrong way, and they don't like it [and] there's friction.*

Q: If you detect something, that the player might not be happy with you, have you ever approached her?

A: *Yeah...I want to know. Yeah, I do [it on the] practice ground or off the course mainly, not on the course...off the course, when we'd finished. Talk can correct it...or try to correct it...but if I can't correct it we part company...I like to stay friends.*

Q: Coz your still going to see them week out and week in?

A: Yeah exactly...and luckily enough all those I've worked for we've...gone out...and it's always been amicable.

Fred has...

A: *Learnt by me mistakes!*

It's important to remember:

A: *I make mistakes, you, the player makes mistakes; as long as you don't blame one another...*

Summary

Aside from a sense of humour, communication is a crucial part of making a good caddy-player relationship effective, according to Fred, where the player is happy to tell the caddy what she likes him to do and they disagree amicably.

Working with a player involves taking responsibility for your own mistakes, not blaming each other. It should be an opportunity to learn. If there are any problems, it is important that the player lets Fred know so that he can do something about it (especially early on in the relationship).

Keeping his Player Confident and Committed

Q: How important do you think it is to make sure your player is confident before she's hitting a shot?
A: *Very important!*
When it comes to boosting her confidence:
A: *[You only do it] fifty percent [of the time], not all the time; just when you feel...she's had a good shot [or she'll] soon get fed up with you....When you can see them sort of coming off the rails a little bit and...maybe getting a little down hearted....I just try and gee them up a little bit.*
Q: Do you see it as part of your role to increase her confidence?
A: *Yeah...well, I wouldn't say to increase her confidence, but to keep her confident...don't let it drop....I mean she's fairly confident going out...but things can go wrong and then that's when you should say something to try and maintain her confidence....Every day's different, every round's different, there's nothing the same.*
Q: How important is it to make sure your player is completely committed to a shot?
A: *Very...one hundred percent. If it's a difficult shot, you give her the options....You've told her what the options are...she made the decision to take the difficult shot on...and you don't want them lashing at it to kill it....'Just keep it smooth,' 'Don't force it'...things like that....She has the choice of alternatives and...she has the final say on everything. You don't try and score points off one another; that's fatal, that's not good.*

137

Summary

Fred considers it vitally important to keep his player confident and committed to a shot. He does this by giving timely words of advice and encouragement.

Player's Goals and Caddy's Role

Q: Does your player set goals for a tournament?
A: *Yes, well she did last week in Tenerife, but that's the first time I've heard her say [so]....Start of the week she said 'we'll go for a top ten this week'....Lot of girls go out and they look at the first two rounds and they're looking at what the cut could be, and they've got that on their minds in the first two rounds. 'What's the cut?'....I never look at the scoreboard [like that]...I do look at the scoreboard but I don't count up. I have an idea what the cut could be, but I'd think...you go out and you do your best...you just give it one hundred percent and do your best and at the end of the day if that's not good enough, that's just too bad....Maybe I'm wrong, maybe I'm right, I don't know, but worrying about numbers doesn't do you any good...a number in your mind is no good. You have a rough idea what it's going to be, so if your borderline, you know if you need a birdie or not...you've a good idea but going out on the golf course with numbers in your mind and worrying about it if you're borderline is not the way to do it I don't think....You should just go and give it one hundred percent and then count up when you come in.*

Knowing his players goals does not make a difference to his performance:
A: *No, I didn't think whatsoever....As far as I'm concerned, we're going out there to be number one...but at the end of the day...we're not. I've got to be realistic and to be honest with you: I know she wasn't. She was looking for a top ten and it wasn't realistic....I mean she don't normally set herself targets, that's unusual...she doesn't normally say that....She has to have [goals]...for herself [to] set some goals....I don't need to know at all, coz as far as I'm concerned I'm going out there to be like I said before, just*

138

to do me, do our best....I don't have finishing positions in mind. I don't have scores in mind. Just go out and give it one hundred percent every day. Just take what comes really. At least you're being honest with yourself....Sometimes when we're on the golf course...we might be two or three over...we'll say...like...'come on, let's try and get this back to level by the end of the day'....Just a little push...just a little pick me up or something.

Q: Do you suggest that or does she say that?

A: *No, me probably...not all the time...if I feel that...we might have had two or three bad holes...and that's it, I just sort of give her, not set her unrealistic targets...like 'oh my God let's get six birdies in seven holes' or something like that...just 'let's try and get three out of the last six holes' or something, a little push.*

Summary

Fred's current player communicated to him her goals for one tournament; a goal that he felt was perhaps unrealistic for her. However, he felt it important for her to have goals and that it ought to not involve a score, nor thinking about the cut (his experience has taught him that this is not helpful). Regardless of what her goals are, he aims to give 100% all the time. He may set a few realistic goals on course to help motivate his player: to help her give her best to the end.

Game Plans

Q: Do you make a game plan together?

A: *Yeah, always...game plan, it'd be course management, really...which is where to lay up where not to lay up...where do you go for carries over water, or things like that.*

Q: And you assess that in...?

A: *[The] practice round....Obviously, things can change; you don't have to stick to it rigidly...because you can get...a hole into the wind one day and downwind the next, so you have to be flexible with your game plan.*

139

Q: Do you know what situations make you change it?

A: *Yeah...really the only time, it's when you've got carries over bunkers or carries over water; if it's into the wind...you wouldn't go for it, you'd lay up...short of the trouble; but if it's downwind, based on the yardage, you change your game plan, coz you can get there in two....You just have to be flexible a bit, but you go out with a game plan....You have to have one...what's the point of all the two practices rounds if you don't make any plans? That's why you have two practice rounds.*

Q: Do you do all the game plan in the first round and then check to see if it works in the second one and refine it or...?

A: *Yeah in the second one...you might see it playing one way one day, but basically...in the two practice rounds you'll examine all sorts of possibilities each time. One time you'll lay up; another time you'll go for it....You've done both...so you know what the alternatives are...so you give yourself alternatives, basically...it's just a different day.*

Q: With a game plan?

A: *You go in there and...you've got something to aim at. You know what you want to do.*

Q: Like little targets?

A: *Yeah every hole...you put it down the left hand side here and then...you've got...your game plan....If it goes well, it's great...but then you've got to adjust it; if it doesn't go well...you might lob one off right and then you've got to re-adjust...but...you need to have some sort of plan...especially when you've got carries over water...you have to eliminate mistakes.*

Summary

Fred always makes a game plan of how they will play the course. This is devised over the two practice rounds where they can try out different alternatives. The plan needs to flexible enough to take into account changes of wind and carries over water. Fred believes it crucial to have a plan before you got out, as it helps eliminate mistakes.

Case Study 4: MIKE PATTERSON

Current player is Karrie Webb.
Other players he has worked with on the LPGA and LET tours include Joanne Morley, Janice Moodie, and Mhairi McKay.

How You Got Into Caddying

A: I use to play a lot. I was a 4 handicap.

After going to university, Mike was looking for a job and since there was a LET event near his home and he knew someone who caddied for a Scottish player he went along. The girl he caddied for then asked him to go to the next event with her. So he did…and 12 years later he is still caddying.

A: My current player and I've… been friends for quite a few years and I've been friends with her old caddy as well, and he retired, and I was kind of in between jobs at the time. Karrie rung me up when I was in Japan working for somebody else…so I decided…yeah.

Q: Did you research your player prior to taking her bag?

A: A little bit yeah. I talked to her old caddy a fair bit, [although] I didn't want to know too much because I wanted to do my own job and not try and emulate what he'd done…You watch her on telly, when you're at tournaments and stuff, so I knew a fair amount about her and we knew each other; not well, but we knew each other okay as friends.

Being a Good Caddy Involves More Than Just a Business Relationship

A: With everybody I've worked for…we've become good friends.

Off the Course

Mike and his players...
A: *Have dinner once a week or once every couple of weeks...and go for a beer or whatever after we've played with them all. In golf, with the players, I think it's important to have an off-the-course relationship as well...because I think that you have to see what each other's like...off the golf course...you know what they're interests are [so] it gives you something to talk about during the round....In Europe...I spent quite a bit more time having dinner with [my player] and stuff off the golf course and stayed at her house and things like that when I was flying back and forth from tournaments, but I don't think there's been a lot of difference really with all...players. I've been quite good friends with them....I think you have...to be friends to an extent...You have to be able to have a laugh, so you have to know each other's senses of humour and I think that's a big thing, but you also have to know when it's time to work and when it's time to focus.*
Mike considers having a friendship with his player advantageous to their working relationship.
Q: What makes a good caddy "good"?
A: *I think it's gelling with your player; I mean...I've always thought you're only really as good as your player....He can have a guy working for a great player who wins loads of golf tournaments and people think that they're a great caddy, but that's not always the case....I think the most important thing for a caddy is when things...aren't going well, and if your player's struggling a little bit, or going though some...harder times than she's perhaps used to...I think...that's the most important time where you can keep your player going....When your player's struggling, that's when the job gets a little harder and that's when you have to work harder caddying.*

On the Course You Need to Know Your Player

A: *I think you need to know your player's personality....I've caddied for players who need...a certain pick up, or who*

*need to be calmed down and I mean…certain players just
need to be…let loose and if they're having a tantrum or
whatever…it's sometimes best just to let them get it off
their chest.*

Q: What you'd say [in response] would vary depending on the
player?

A: *Depending on the player and their personality….I've learnt
by my mistakes, so…I found that to calm a player down
when they don't need it…sometimes you just need to get
it off your chest and that only comes through knowing a
player.*

Q: Do you discuss the effectiveness of your relationship with
your players?

A: *Every now and again…I can't know where I stand, unless
she tells me I've done a good job on that day [although] I
know pretty well when I've made a mistake or anything
like that.*

Summary

Having a good relationship with your player, which is like a
friendship, is advantageous, according to Mike. It helps you
to know how your player will react in certain situations and
gives you topics to talk about between shots on the course.
This friendly working relationship is a good foundation in
which both player and caddy can be comfortable enough to
discuss the effectiveness of their relationship.

Role of Player Versus Caddy

A: *Ultimately…the player's the boss and you can't tell
them…what to do; you can only make a suggestion
about…what you think you should maybe do. I mean, I
would never tell a player to do something…they don't
need to be told what to do and…that's why they're
professional golfers and…I'm not; it's coz they know what
to do and I can…only help to…a certain degree….The
player's got the final call.*

Summary

Mike has a very clear understanding of his player's roles in their relationship, relative to his own role. At the end of the day the player is the number one decision maker.

The Caddy's Role: The Standard and Practical Side

A: Most of the players I've worked for have never had to fire caddies or anything like that; it's just been something that's happened….It gives me obviously a standard which I have to live up to, because if they've never fired a caddy, their caddy before has obviously been good….I have to prove to them that I can do as good a job as their other caddies.

The ~~Scout's~~ Caddy's motto: "BE PREPARED." Mike's role includes…

A: Making sure that everything is ready for play each morning. Make sure we've got enough balls, gloves, food in the bag and rain gear….Make sure I know what the weather forecast is, wind direction…coz that way I have compass points in the yardage book….[I'd] rather carry…than forget the [rain] trousers….On the golf course…make your player as comfortable as possible; make sure they've all got the information that they'll need; and as I said to you…as a caddy you never ever want to say 'I don't know'….So when I'm…at a golf course on a Monday, walking the golf course with my yardage book, I have to look for possible situations we might get into, and how to get out of them in the best way possible….If I think a player is about to do something wrong…I think that's one of the most important things a caddy does is: stops a player making mistakes.

Processing and Communicating Information

A: I'll get to the ball and give her [the] yardage. What it is to the front, what it is to the flag…and then what it is over bunkers, short of bunkers, or whatever…and that's pretty much all I'll say; and then, from then on it's up to my

144

player to ask me questions...above and beyond that, about how far it's actually playing, what the wind's doing, is it uphill or downhill?

Q: So if they want more information, you'll tell them?

A: *Yes....I've got that information right in my head, coz I know what...I'm about to be asked....The worst thing a caddy can ever say is 'I don't know'....You've got to have an answer, and...it better be right most of the time....I will have an idea...basically as soon as I get a number, I'll know pretty much its gonna be one of two clubs...and then I start thinking about why one club would be better than the other, and...we talk all the way through about each shot....She'll ask me questions and...I'll ask her questions....All I'll do is give a yardage and a wind direction and then my player will ask me questions from there...about how far something is playing, where we need to land it, where trouble is....Do we want to miss it here, y'know, the best place to miss it if...that was going to have to be the case....It's important to know how much of the information you compute, you actually volunteer, to your player.*

Mike's exact thoughts go something like this:

A: *Well we've got a hundred and fifty to the front, the pin's fifteen on, that's one sixty-five's our total....I'll say it's what the wind's doing: say...it's playing three yards into the wind...so that makes our total one sixty-eight, but it's more downhill, so that's one sixty-four....That's what it's playing to the pin and we have to land it [there] coz the greens are releasing six to seven yards short, so that's where we want to land it. It's playing one fifty-seven. Which would be, for example...a great six iron....That's more my thought process...because I would never tell...unless I'm asked... 'what club do you think?' or...she'll always make the suggestion, and then...I'll say yes, no, y'know, whatever....[With] the players I've worked for...you get into a routine of how you talk about a shot and...as I've said to you...I've always had my way of doing things but that's...had to change around players and how...they want things done....Some players like to take more responsibility themselves [and] some players…might put more responsibility on the caddy.*

It's Important to be Consistent and Upbeat Emotionally

A: *I think you just have to…be exactly the same all the time, and…you've always got to have confidence in your player and show your player that you've got confidence in them, because…if they're struggling or whatever, they don't need to see their caddy…dragging along twenty yards behind them looking…disappointed at the way things are going and looking…like a caddy who doesn't have trust in their player. I mean that's possibly the worst thing a caddy can do, I would have said….I think most players, all they really want is somebody who…can be calm under pressure….When you're…tied for the lead, with four holes to go in a major…you're no different to…the way you were when you teed off on the first day of that major…..Just don't show that you're nervous.*

Feeling and Dealing with Emotions

A: *I'm not sure about other caddies, but…I certainly feel a little bit nervous…in certain situations….I think that's natural; I think it's good to feel that way to an extent….Sometimes [I] feel…a few butterflies; I wouldn't say it was nervousness, more just a few butterflies…before you tee off in the final group on a Sunday….I think that's perfectly natural….I think I hide it [well], or that's what I've been told anyway….I think you always have to be pretty much on a level [emotionally]…not get really high or really, really low. I mean a player doesn't need to see…their caddy jumping around….Just have the same aura about yourself…whether it's… on a Thursday morning or whether it's the Sunday afternoon…whether your player's made a double or made an eagle.*

Q: So, you need consistency of personality or behaviour; is that it?

A: Yes….Your player doesn't want to see you…down and depressed; [they] don't need to see that coming from their caddy….A player who's trying to win a tournament doesn't need to be calming their caddy down!…I think that's pretty good for a caddy who can stay just level.

Summary

The role of a caddy, according to Mike, involves being organised enough to have all the practical needs of the player met including equipment, food, and appropriate clothing. It involves getting the numbers right and knowing the course intimately so that you are the "knowledge" for your player. Furthermore, caddies are required to be stable and an emotional rock for their players, regardless of how they might be feeling inside or what is going on with your players.

An Effective Caddy-Player Relationship Involves Trust: The Player Needs to Trust the Caddy

A: They have to have complete trust in your numbers and…your lines….You wouldn't be working for them very long, if they didn't trust you….Most players know within a week…if it's going to work or not….If the caddy makes a good decision…that a player didn't necessarily think was the right decision at the start, and he hit[s] the shot, trust[s] the caddy; it probably only takes one incident…one situation where the caddy says 'no this is right, trust me,' and they do and it comes off that's …

Q: …one way to make the relationship more concrete?

A: Yes, I think so, yes.

Another sign that a player trusts her caddy:

A: When you're on the driving range practising, and they start to tell you about what they're working on in their swing, and say, look at things, and…that's quite a big thing for a player because their coach is…their main set of eyes, and once they bring the caddy into it, to look at little bits and pieces about their swing then….I think that's when the trust is starting.

There are many factors that can influence a player and her ability to trust her caddy:

A: *Probably a little bit...natural to be a little harder to trust somebody else when you've never had to do it before.*

Q: So it can depend on the player's experience of caddies?

A: *Yeah....If...a player's had some bad experiences with caddies, it might take longer....It takes a little bit of time, [as a player], to build up a certain amount of trust in your caddy....Once you've made a few good calls, then that's when players will start to trust you more; but obviously, if you['re] making a couple of mistakes, that's when that trust maybe starts to...go back just that little bit; but...it's your job to build that trust back up again.*

It's a Two-way Street: As a Caddy, You Also Need to Trust Your Player

A: *I think they have to trust you a lot, too...listen to you when you're trying to stop them from doing something where you think they're gonna make a mistake....You also have to trust your player that she knows, too, that...caddies make mistakes sometimes and...bring trouble into play, and whatever, which doesn't need to be done. But the player can stop the caddy and that's when it works well together, when you can stop each other...making mistakes....If I'm uncertain about something, I would tell the player I was uncertain about it....Sometimes a player will just say 'you know, this is my call; here this is what I like.' It takes a while to get to know a player, to know that they can hit certain shots and...on different golf courses. Even if it's windy or bouncy or whatever, there can be three or four different...shots of which...to consider; you won't always agree...but, you have to make sure that the player knows what they're doing and...that's just when you have to let them go sometimes.*

Q: So it's like trusting your player as well?

A: *Yeah.*

Q: Not just them trusting you, but you, trusting them?

A: *Exactly, yeah.*

Summary

Trust is crucial to the player-caddy relationship. The player needs to be able to trust the caddy, especially his numbers and lines. It takes a while for a player to trust a caddy, but there are a few things that will make the difference and that you can look out for that shows that your player has developed trust in you. Trust is a two-way street, where the caddy also needs to trust the player and her final call on a situation. Regardless of the situation, the caddy needs to appear that he is confident and trusts his player's ability to perform at all times.

Confidence and Commitment of the Player

Q: How important is it to make sure your player is confident before playing a shot?

A: *Very important...that's not always the case on each day, that the player is one hundred percent confident, but that's what most caddies aim to have: their player's complete confidence, even if it ends up being wrong....It's better to have a player trusting what their doing....Make sure they're standing over a shot knowing what they're doing is right.*

Q: Do you see it as part of your role to increase a player's confidence?

A: *Yes...because I think golf's a game that's...based on confidence....There's players who...aren't necessarily as good a ball strikers as other players out there, but they're supremely confident in what they're doing....I think that's just the...best thing for players to have is confidence. And [it] often...comes and goes very quickly.*

Q: How important is it for you to make sure your player is completely committed to her shot?

A: *Very important...you have to make sure that what they're doing is going to be right...you can't let them have any doubts in their mind about what they're about to do.*

Mike considers the difference between confidence and commitment:

A: I think…that confidence is something that is more long lasting [whereas] by committing to the shot, I mean…just for those wee seconds leading up to it, [is about] putting a swing on it. I think…when I talk about committing to the shot, it's putting the best swing on it as possible.

Q: How do you ensure that a player is completely committed to a shot?

A: By making sure they have the right information and…never umming and arhing about what you're…suggesting that they do…and…just sounding confident…yourself about what…they have to do.

Q: How do you ensure that a player is confident?

A: I never want to sound doubtful myself; I never want sound as if I'm guessing.

Summary

To Mike, it's important to have your player's full confidence in both his abilities as a caddy, and the shot at hand. If he has this from his player, then they are more likely to commit to the shot. One of the best ways he can gain his player's confidence in the task at hand is by sounding confident himself.

Communicating With Your Player: "Caddy-talk"

Q: How regularly would you discuss the effectiveness of your caddy-player relationship?

A: Could be…a couple of weeks, once a week. I might not talk about it for a couple of months; it just depends on how things are going.

Q: Do you think it's beneficial?

A: Yep….I think you have to be kept on your toes, as a caddy, I mean you can't ever get too comfortable when you're in your job….Once you feel too comfortable, that's when you're in trouble, you have to always think that…it's one more mistake and this could be me….A lot of what I say isn't stuff I've planned to say….I think once you start planning to say things, it sounds fake and...sounds unnatural.

Q: How do you know when to say what?

A: *Just through experience, I think...[I've] said...the right things at the right time, but I think that only comes through saying the wrong things at the wrong time....I've learnt through my mistakes.*

Q: What is it that separates a top caddy from an average caddy?

A: *I think the caddies that actually speak their mind...to their player, and stop their player from making mistakes, I think that's the sign of a good caddy.....People who just agree with their players, they probably...get themselves into trouble...I don't think that's something that's ever...*

Q: ...recommended?

A: *Because people start...realising...all they really want is somebody who'll...speak their mind.*

Between Shots

A: *We just talk about everything....We just talk about...life, and sport, and y'know...we talk about absolutely everything. She knows as much about me as I know about her....[We're] confidants in each other...at times, and you both need that.*

When Preparing for a Shot

A: *We start off obviously with the yardage, then we look for trouble areas; and if we can avoid trouble, where would be best and what we should steer away from....A week like this [The Women's British Open], you have to steer away from trouble a lot more than you do in a regular week in America, where you just fire it at the flag the whole time....We just talk about staying out of trouble more than anything....I will have an idea, I mean basically, as soon as I get a number I'll know pretty much [that] it's gonna be one of two clubs...and then I start thinking about why one club would be better than the other and...we talk all the way through about each*

151

*shot….She'll ask me questions, and… I'll ask her
questions….I give the facts and then I can always tell if
she's happy or unhappy with my suggestions and she'll
make a suggestion or…if we disagree…ultimately I have
to make her realise that what she's about to do is
absolutely a hundred percent correct….If there is a little
bit of doubt in my mind, I have to make her believe it's
absolutely right, as she can't go into a shot thinking
'this…maybe isn't right' and I'd rather a player put a good
swing on it…and end up being slightly wrong, than put a
bad swing on it when it could have been right….You have
[to] get…them confident, complete confidence walking
into a shot, I think.*

Q: Specifically?

A: *We talk about how far it's actually playing….We've got a
yardage of one hundred and fifty, then we take hill and
wind…if it's uphill/downhill into account. This one hundred
and fifty yardage could be playing one sixty-two…with
wind and slightly uphill, then we have to work out where
we have to land it if the greens are releasing. I'll never
say to her what club I think it is; I'll tell her what I think the
yardage is…and then she'll suggest to me a club…or
she'll ask what do you think….I would never say…what
club to hit.*

Q: What if she might say, 'oh I don't know, what do you
think?'

A: *Then I would tell her….All I'll do is give a yardage and a
wind direction and then my player will ask me questions
from there…about how far something is playing, where
we need to land it, where trouble is…do we want to miss
it here, y'know, the best place to miss it if…that was going
to have to be the case….I would never tell…unless I'm
asked…what club do you think, or…she'll always make
the suggestion, and then we, I'll say yes, no…whatever.*

The decision-making process is a bit more difficult if the
player doesn't think the same way as the caddy:

A: *If we have to take a three iron off a tee, and she'll say to
me 'why aren't I hitting driver?' and I'll say to
her…'There's…[a] bunker out here at two-fifty or…there's
no point in us even getting close to [it] because we'll only*

152

have a eight iron or seven iron, if we hit three iron'....There's no point in taking unnecessary risks....I never tell her 'there's out of bounds here, and there's a lake over there, and...this is the fairway you have to hit it.'

Q: What would you say if you agree with the shot choice?

A: *[I] would just tell them...that was what you were thinking...again [it's] just that confidence thing, and commitment thing, about telling them this is right...this is what we've agreed on [it] is absolutely right....You always discuss things and...they'll tell you 'do you like this?'...and if you like it, then every time you like it, make sure they know...that...it's the right choice, because...you don't want to be seen to be saying 'yeah that's fine' all the time....If I disagree with their choice...I wouldn't tell them it's wrong. I would say to them well, maybe let's just consider this option...because this is the way I see it....I know where all the trouble is on the golf course, but you don't need to be telling your player where...the trouble is because they don't want to be seeing trouble all the time....If they're in between clubs, and we've gone for a longer club...there's a lake just off the back edge of the green, then I'll explain...maybe we should just try and hit the shorter club and see what happens and take the back...of the green out of play....If I think a player is about to do something wrong, I mean...that's one of the most important things a caddy does is stop a player making mistakes.*

The "Switch on and Switch off" Transition

A: *Once you get to the ball, that's when you have [to] start thinking about what you have to do...so you have to know when to draw the line of having fun and business.*

Q: How do you know when to draw that line?

A: *I think you just learn with your player....I know that ten, fifteen yards before we reach the ball, it's time to start thinking about the shot. I will cut conversation off just about before we reach the ball, coz the last thing a player needs is her caddy yapping away when...you get to the ball and he hasn't got a yardage or anything like that…..Just before you get to the ball; that's when you have to start thinking about what you have to do about the next shot so…I often just say something…like…maybe you need to start concentrating now.*

What to Say When Things are Going Well

A: *You just try and keep the same momentum going…just keep doing…everything exactly the same as you were…doing…coz it might [get you] out of [a] certain routine that you're in that makes her play well.*

Q: Okay, so whatever you've been saying before, you'll keep saying that kind of thing?

A: *Yeah exactly….I've always tried to get my players relaxed and…talk[ing] about…anything apart from golf…in between shots.*

What to Say if Things are Going Badly

A: *If things are going badly we might try and change something…maybe approach…a shot differently. Maybe you have to be a little more aggressive, or things might be going badly, because you're too aggressive, and it's time to slow things down a little bit and think a little bit more clearly about what you have to do….Maybe tell them to slow down a little bit or just to maybe think about…maybe a small thing in their golf swing….If they're not playing too well…there can be a lack of trust in what they're doing…they have to…start trusting…what they're doing, trusting the shot, and seeing the shot a little better…and connecting to the shot….When players aren't playing well, there is a certain amount of…hesitancy there…and it's a matter of trusting what you're doing and…committing to things….Every player I've worked for… always believed that if there's a hole out there, there's a chance of making a birdie. So, I would…try and say, if we're not having such a good day, that we've got enough holes left to turn it around into a respectable day….I would say to a player that…if we're having a bad*

*first round it's a matter of getting it in [and] working on
things so we can get things going for the last three days.*
When communicating Mike says remember:
*A: I always want to sound totally confident in what I'm
doing...that's what I want to do, sound as confident as
possible, and tell them that what we're doing is
not...going to get us in any trouble what-so-ever, because
you always want them to do the best thing that they've
got, onto each shot.*

Summary

Talking to his player is a big part of Mike's job as a caddy.
This includes assessing the effectiveness of their
relationship, dealing with mistakes, preparing for each shot,
keeping his player positive when it's going badly, and keeping
the momentum when it's going well. Sounding confident in
the manner in which he communicates at all times is crucial.
Knowing when to say what has come from experience of
making mistakes.

Making Mistakes and Learning in the Lifespan of a Caddy-player Relationship: A Caddy Can Often "Live or Die" by His Mistakes

*A: You can't ever get too comfortable when you're in your
job....Once you feel too comfortable, that's when you're in
trouble; you have to always think that...it's one more
mistake and this could be me.*
However, a variety of factors can cause a player-caddy
relationship to come to an end:
*A: [One player] wasn't particularly happy being in the States,
coz it was just the start of being over there after playing
Europe, and I think both relationships just really got a little
bit stale....When you go through good times and bad
times, and it gets to the extent where everything is the
same everyday (and players don't always like that),
maybe you need a little spark to...get them going
again....So [my previous caddy jobs had] nothing to do
with the job I was doing, [they] just [needed] something*

155

fresh and something new and that can make a big difference for a player.

Making a Mistake is Fine if you Learn from it the First Time

A: I learnt something yesterday….Everyday you learn something different, because every situation's different so…if you're in that situation again, you can look back and think 'well we were in that situation and this is what we did and it was right or wrong or whatever.' If it was wrong, you have to make sure its right the second time.

Q: Would you say you make fewer mistakes now than when you did when you first started caddying?

A: Oh yeah, definitely.

Mike and his players know how to best deal with mistakes:

A: Sometimes I've had bad days, sometimes she has bad days, and we try…and make it so that neither of us have a bad day on the same day…so we can rescue each other….We're out practising…she'll…tell me look y'know, we've got to stop doing this, or we've got to think a little bit more in these situations.

Every day and every experience is an opportunity to learn:

A: I think…one of the easiest ways to learn is just by actually doing it….I think you can only learn by being in the actual situation….I'm still learning…from every single time I go out on a golf course…and I watch other caddies and see what they do (and [that is] the guys that you have respect for out there) and…the players that you have respect for and how…certain other players and caddies work together….The guys you watch when they work, [the] guys who were out there when I first came out…you'd just be watching them and what they did in certain situations, has helped me.

Q: So would you recommend that if someone was learning to be a caddy…that she would watch some of…the better caddies in action?

A: Yeah.

Summary

Making mistakes is an integral part of being a caddy for Mike. However, it's important to learn from these mistakes.
Learning the first time round is important, as the nature of the job is very transient.

Player and Caddy Goals: His Goals as a Caddy

A: Other than trying to win, that's the only…
Q: Goal?
A: Yeah, and winning's not necessarily a goal; its just a…
Q: …an outcome?
A: Yeah exactly, I mean, I can't see my goal this week is to win, because if you don't win then if you finish second is it a bad week? Of course not, that's the thing, I mean that's why I don't think you can really set…goals for each week, coz if you don't quite achieve them, then… it could be seen as a bad week.

Mike's Player's goals:

A: She sets goals for herself.
Q: Are you ever made aware of these?
A: Yep.
Q: Do you think it's beneficial or useful for you to know what her goals are?
A: No, not really; she keeps most of them very much to herself…she doesn't need to be telling people, and telling the press…what her goals are for the year; she keeps them to herself and I know just one or two.
Q: Do you and your players ever set goals or make a game plan together prior to going out to play?
A: Certain weeks we have a game plan, like this week, U.S. Open week, we have…coz weeks where you don't need to go really low under par to win… you have [to] avoid trouble and…that's when we set more goals. Most weeks in America, it's hit it at the flag, and hole the putts, and you have to get to twenty under par to win a tournament, so…it's difficult to…set a goal for the week when it's

twenty under to win. You've just gotta go out and make
birdies and that's that.

Q: So only when it's not "stock standard" you'll perhaps
   discuss it…like this week: to keep out of trouble?

A: *Yeah, just [on] difficult golf courses….I walk the golf*
   course on the Monday that I always…look for trouble
   when I am walking a golf course. So if we get into trouble,
   I know how to get out of it, and how to stay away from
   trouble, whether it's an easy golf course or a difficult golf
   course….Sometimes, good to know what the goals are,
   but I don't think of it really makes that much of a
   difference in the working relationship, whether you knew
   what those goals were or not I mean…ultimately…you
   can only help them to a certain extent.

Summary

Mike doesn't set any outcome goals for each round; however,
he does set process goals—making sure he has a game plan
on how best to play each hole, even if they get into trouble.
This becomes a stock standard goal in the States, because
the courses are usually very similar. He knows his player sets
goals, but doesn't think he needs to know what they are, in
order for him to carry out his job effectively.

Case Study 5: ANONYMOUS TOUR CADDY

He has worked with winning players on the LPGA and LET tours.
He had also caddied in the Solheim Cup and placed in the top three in a major.

Becoming a Caddy: Beginnings and Endings and Learning the Ropes

Q: How long have you been working as a caddy?

A: *Years; I guess...nine.*

Q: How did you get into caddying?

A: *Just through [one player]; she...lives in my home town and [I] started with her; she's...yeah, basically took me over to America first couple of times...*

Q: And corrupted you?

A: *Corrupted me, exactly right. It's a good lifestyle...good fun, and yeah I enjoy it.*

Q: How long did you work with her [your initial player]?

A: *Six and a half years. And then...odd weeks here and there; I've worked for quite a few different girls.*

Q: With this initial player?

A: *I'm a family friend and she knew me so...she basically took me out, taught me...just learning on the job isn't it? I suppose [it's] like work experience...you pick it up as you go after a few years.*

Q: Was she a good teacher?

A: *Yeah [she] was good [because] she's real easy to communicate with... but...as for picking up caddying skills, you just sort of pick it up as you go along....[She] taught me that.*

Q: How did...your relationship with [your initial player] come to an end?

A: *It was more my doing, coz I was just ready for a change...and...she hadn't being playing that well and I was ready for change anyway....[She] was injured as well at the time, she had a wrist injury. I went and caddied for*

159

[my current player] for a couple of weeks...and got on...well with her and yeah that's how I asked [her] and that was it.

Q: So you actually asked [her]?

A: Yeah.

Q: How long have you been working with [your current player]?

A: Eighteen months.

Caddy–player Relationship: Friendship and Matching of Personalities

Q: How would you describe your working relationship with her [your current player]?

A: Very good...relaxed atmosphere for the most part...yeah, easy to get on with...easy going, same sort of...senses of humour, so it's pretty easy.

Q: How would you say you worked together?

A: Quite good...with the occasional douze up....We've got similar interests...sports and stuff like...that sort of thing. I think...you gotta be more of a friend out there on the course than anything; that's the biggest thing, I reckon if you gonna caddy for someone, you gotta be a friend with them as well....[It's] very important...you can't have chalk and cheese out there....I don't see her much off the golf course to be honest....I go to dinner with her every now and then, I suppose, but it's more with [her] on the golf course so...

Q: [It's] very professional?

A: Yeah.

Summary

Having a relaxed atmosphere between him and his player is important. Part of caddying is being a friend—although this is a friendship that is largely restricted to the golf course.

Building Trust with his Players

Q: How long did it take for you to build trust with her [your initial player]?

A: *Not long at all coz we were instantly [there]....I'm a family friend and she knew me, so she was always going to trust in me.*

Q: Has your [current] player developed trust in you, do you think?

A: *Yeah...I think [so].*

Q: At what point in your relationship did that really kick in?

A: *After I've started working for her, two or three weeks I suppose. After...she realised...that I could do the job for her and then we just developed a bond.*

Q: How did you know she trusted you at that point?

A: *Well, you don't know but...she's got to trust me...coz I'm giving her her yardage. I mean she has to trust me....I'm sure she probably looks over my shoulder when I'm giving her the yardage. She probably...checks it's the right number but...at the end of the day she trusts me; but how do I know...well...it's hard to say.*

Q: What factors do you think build trust in a player-caddy relationship?

A: *Just like doing the little things, y'know...e.g., turning up on time; like if she says 'I want you to be there at five-thirty in the morning for a practice round' and if your not there at five-thirty, that's straight away, [she's] not going to trust me...so little things like that.*

Q: Have you ever been late before?

A: *Yeah once before.*

Q: Due to faults of your own or...?

A: *Yeah, it was quite funny...once for eight years, so I think that's pretty good....I could have been late this morning actually the traffic coming here...the traffic's terrible this morning....If I'm told eight o'clock, you always get there at least ten minutes before eight o'clock...always allow a little extra time....You gotta have trust, coz if you haven't got trust, then your player is going to be doubting herself, so you gotta have trust; it's probably closer to a one hundred [percent] trust...one hundred percent [important]....It's not a difficult role, it's just pretty much turn up, turn up in time, be on time always....But it's an important role...at the end of the day we're giving out yardages for the girls and...they trust us...they trust our judgments. Like…you could be anything between a seven and an eight iron and it comes down to the last hole of a tournament; say the caddy says a seven iron and the player's thinking eight iron…it makes a big difference…that's where the trust comes back into it again…coz if they don't trust you and trust your views…there's no point in being out there.*

Summary

This caddy considers trust to be a very important element in a player-caddy relationship. The player needs to trust the caddy and his yardages. One way to help develop trust with your player is to ensure you pay attention to the small things, like getting there on time.

Job Security and Relationship Effectiveness

Knowing what makes a good caddy-player relationship is the first step:

Q: What makes a good player-caddy relationship?

A: Well that's a fine line.…I mean [with] a successful golfer everyone assumes they have a good relationship [with their caddy]…but what makes it, I don't know.…Just personality I guess…apart from…doing a fairly good job for them…you got to do that as well that's…a big part of it.

Q: What exactly is doing a good job, in your definition?

A: It's…just little things…like being prompt and…making sure everything's alright on the golf course and yardage wise…but basically being professional.…[With my first player]…coz I'm a family friend, I guess…just that's the slightly different aspect, like I could sort of…get away with more with [her] like…if I had of turned up late or something silly like that.…But with [my current player] it's [like a] player-caddy working relationship would be with [her]…y'know, [she's] quite probably tough on me, I suppose.

Q: So [your current player's] quite a little bit more down the line; is that what you're trying to say?
A: *Yeah, which is a good thing.*
Q: Do you ever discuss the effectiveness of your relationship?
A: *No....It can't be a good thing....I mean we're getting along quite well, I think, so there's no reason to discuss the past.*
Q: So it could be more of an option?
A: *How we could improve our relationship? I suppose that'd be the question. What we would do....But I think we get on pretty well, so we don't need...to do it....If a player and a caddy are discussing...their relationship, it'd be a bad thing, I think, coz if there's any discussion, usually there'd be something's wrong.*
Q: You didn't sit down and...say 'hey, am I still employed for the next year or...?'
A: *That's a long time for longevity; no I mean this job's...you're here today, done tomorrow sort of thing; you don't know.*
Q: So you don't necessarily formally discuss your...?
A: *Future? No. Like for the moment everything's rosy...and that's pretty much the way it is. It's just basically contract work...week by week.*

Summary

Knowing what makes a good relationship—having the right personalities and doing all the small things well—is crucial in creating an effective caddy-player relationship, according to this caddy. Discussing the effectiveness of his relationship with his player has been synonymous with things going badly in the past.

The Caddy's Role and Logistics: Essential Qualities of a Caddy

Q: If you had the chance to train a caddy, what skills would you suggest s/he would need to acquire?

A: *Positive attitude and communication skills; excellent knowledge of golf and dedication to the job.*

Q: What is it that separates a top caddy from an average caddy?

A: *Dedication and attention to detail. 'Thick skin' is an essential quality for a caddy. When you've got a fiery player, you've gotta be...really thick skinned. I mean you're a caddy, you've got to let it go straight over the top of your head, because if you get a fiery player, often they will take any...anger, I guess...out on the caddy, whether its the caddy's fault or not. Might be but basically...you're there; you're the punching bag at times....I've never really worked [for] any players like that and I don't know if I [could work with someone like that] long term...probably like...a really successful player, I suppose...but if it was somebody that's...plodding along, no! There's gotta be something in it for the caddy...there's no point smashing your head against a wall.*

Learning from Other Caddies

Going out on tour this caddy learnt many things, not just from his player, but from other caddies.

A: *When I first started...things like that, I never knew before I started...pitches and...like the distances; how far it pitches and how far it releases on the greens and little stuff like that.*

Q: So you record all of that when you out there?

A: *Yeah...and grain, and where the grain goes when you got that on the greens...all that sort of stuff....I didn't really know about that until I was out there.*

Summary

Being a good caddy involves a variety of skills including being positive and a good communicator. Dealing with fiery players requires the ability to have 'thick skin' and not take it personally. According to this caddy, attention to detail is what separates the best caddies from the mediocre, and much of this can be learnt out on tour (such as recording a player's pitch and release on greens).

Making Your Player Confident

Q: How important is it to make sure your player...is confident before playing a shot?
A: *Yeah, very important.*
Q: Is that your job? Is that your responsibility?
A: *Yeah, it is like you'll hear....I always give her a target. I think that maybe I have helped [her] a little bit in her focus on the golf course like...when I first started caddying for her; her coach had mentioned to me that she had accidentally lost her focus when she shouldn't. 'Get on your target,' like that's what the Americans say 'get on your target,' 'get focused,' and all this. And so every tee shot now I give her a target and...every time I say 'on that, y'know, tree' or what ever it is...on that target; and I do that all the time now, so....Whether that's good or not, I think it's given her a little bit extra focus, rather than just getting up there and just looking at the fairway....To her confidence, it's gotta help just reinforcing in the back of her mind...what she's...wanting to do, target.*
Q: How do you ensure that she's confident before playing a shot?
A: *If it's like when we spoke earlier, I s'pose sorting a club....If you're between a seven and an eight iron and she's doubtful...you've gotta [in]stil confidence [in a] way saying 'this is the iron because this is what' y'know...this is why it's a seven iron. It's not the eight iron because of that other reason, whatever that was. That's the way to get confidence. Hopefully she'll get over the ball and [be confident].*
Q: So you provide the logic, in other words?
A: *Just reason, yeah.*
Q: How important is it to you that a player is confident all the time?
A: *Quite important; I mean one hundred [percent].*
Q: Do you see it as...your role to increase her confidence?

A: *Yeah, should be more, it is a role, but how much of a role we can play; I dunno. I mean... it is quite a major role.*

Q: How do you go about ensuring that your player is confident?

A: *By showing faith in them and be[ing] positive at all times.*

Q: How important is it to you that a player is confident before playing?

A: *Extremely!*

Q: Do you see it as part of your role to increase her confidence?

A: *Yes, [because] if they are not confident, it can reflect in their game.*

Q: How important is it to make sure your player is completely committed to her shot?

A: *Very important!*

Q: How do you ensure that she is completely committed to her shot?

A: *Remove all distractions and help her focus on the task at hand.*

Summary

To this caddy, it is vitally important that he makes his player confident and committed on every shot and he helps to do this by highlighting the target—something positive for her to focus on. He also reinforces the chosen club with reasons why it is the right club, and is generally positive and displays faith in his player at all times.

Conversations: Over Choosing a Club

A: *We discuss all shots until we can agree on a suitable choice.*

Q: So if [she is] thinking 'it's an eight iron...it's the last hole of a tournament,' your thinking 'seven iron'; what do you do? How do you bring it up?

A: *Well you tell her 'I think it's a seven iron' because of whatever reasons, y'know, 'it's uphill,' 'its downhill,' or...'y'know, the wind's here; that's why it's a seven iron, it's not an eight iron'....You gotta have a reason...like if*

it's either or, you gotta say…why…you can't really [just]
say 'seven iron.'

Q: What input do you have in helping your player in choosing
   a particular shot to play?

A: *[I'm] very influential.*

Q: What information do you provide?

A: *Club selection, weather conditions, yardage, [and] green*
   reads.

Q: Once a player decides on a shot, what do you do?

A: *Tell her to go for it and be aggressive and positive.*

Q: Do you convey your thoughts on the shot choice?

A: *Always…. [I do this] directly. There needs to be no mince*
   words as this may lead to confusion.

Summary

This caddy and his player always discuss shots. He will give
reasons when he doesn't agree with the player's choice in
club, and then he will encourage her over the shot. He
believes in communicating directly so that there is no
confusion.

The Good and the Bad: Knowing When to Say What

A: *If they're playing well, yeah just [say] little things….If she*
   hits a good shot, [say] 'great shot there,' 'great swing,'
   just little things…just reinforce her…just get her
   confidence up…. If things are going badly, well again, you
   gotta try and somehow get her out of thinking negatively
   by…maybe giving her some sort of…swing thought or
   something to work on…just to get her round the golf
   course without doing too much damage. Just like…one
   time, I don't know where it was, but she was swinging
   bad. I could see what she was doing in her swing, so I
   just said 'Y'know what? You[‘re] doing this.' I said…she
   was just coming up off the ball…and hanging behind. I
   said 'you're just…y'know, falling back, but just stay on top
   of the ball'… It's just little things like that…just gives her
   something to think about rather than thinking negatively;
   it's a positive thought…and…hopefully it'll sort of stop the

bleeding out there on the golf course....How do I know when to say what? Well that just comes with experience, I think. After eight years you sort of know…when to push the buttons....Like y'know, she needs a kick in the bum, you gotta say 'come on pull your head in'….You just know when to say things and when not to.

Q: At what point in your career did you learn this?

A: Pretty early…you pick that up over…maybe six months…pretty much half way through your first year you realise, okay. Even earlier, I'd say early. I'd give it a month; you sorta… know when to shut up and when not to…pretty much…it's just…knowing her….Y'know, knowing what she's thinking…just reading between the lines… You've got to read what she's thinking….I know if she has a double bogey, let's say, and she's really, really pissed off, and…I can see her that she's pissed off…and there is no point, you can't play golf like that, and [on] the next holes…you just gotta try and cut it out.

Summary

This caddy likes to keep his players positive at all times, when playing well or not-so-well. This involves knowing when is the right time to say things, which is something that he learns in the first month of working with a player (from observing them).

Talking Between Shots and When in Contention.

Q: What things do you talk to your player about during a round?

A: Oh, anything from…sport, politics…and anything in between….There's just talking about different things, I suppose…we've got similar interests…sports and stuff…just that sort of thing.

Q: Does she like talking?

A: Yeah.

Q: Do you like talking?

A: Yeah, I don't mind….During a tournament you don't tend to talk so much when you're in contention…which is just

really silly...when you think about it. Thursday,
Fridays...you're more relaxed and 'how ya going' sort a
thing...and when it comes down to the crunch time in the
weekends, you don't sorta [do] much talking. What we
say it's probably the same, I don't remember much.

Q: Why do you think it's probably silly when it comes down to
it?

A: *Well you should be...just yourself, no matter what [if] it is*
Thursday or Sunday.

Q: Do you think it would perhaps make her play better if
you...kept talking?

A: *Yes...I'd try to do that, like if she was in contention on*
Sunday, and she seemed like she was getting a bit tense,
I'd sorta try to cool her down a little bit by saying
'hey...did you watch the cricket last night?' Y'know,
obviously [you try to] get her mind get off...thinking about
the tournament...just try and relax her.

Summary

Between shots they like to talk about their common interests,
such as another sport like cricket. In some self-realisation, he
feels that they don't talk as much as they ought to when in
contention on the final day, that they need to keep the
amount of conversation the same as during the first round.

Preparing for a Round and in Reflection Afterwards

Q: What do you talk to her about during practice, or before
and after a round?

A: *During practice, just little things like just work[ing] on her*
game. Swing techniques and stuff.

Q: Do you help her with that?

A: *Yeah, I pass on a little bit, through her coach in America*
I've sort of picked up [on] her faults...sorta see what she's
doing wrong sorta thing [and] that there's no problems
there...

Q: Does she rely on you if the coach isn't around?

A: *A little bit yeah...it's good; I think it's good coz [it's a] little*
bit of input that you can have. Of course...these days,

with videos and video cameras, you sort of put it on a video, download it and send it to the coach anyway...but I mean I can notice little things anyway in her swing as well as anyone else, so yeah it's good...it's pretty important....Before...a tournament round...when she gets to a tournament place...that's when...she starts concentrating...so she'll sorta go into her own...shell...and...go to the range and she'll focus. It's different on practice days...there'd be less talk...in tournament days...when I say less talk....You go to like practice days and everyone's sorta relaxed...you just talk to other people on the range, but on [a] tournament day, you go to the range and do your practice and get out.

Q: So you're a lot more task focused?

A: *Yeah, that's it...more focused at the end of the day....Good point. Your practice should be focused as well; so not good isn't it? Don't get into that! No point practising unless you're putting a hundred percent into what you've practiced... After a tournament round? What do we talk about? Well you just analyse what went wrong and what was good and just focus on the good things and not the bad things. But you always want to look at your faults...so that you can improve on it...and just...go to the range and try to find it [your swing] again.*

Q: Do you always analyse the round?

A: *Not always no...well fifty percent [of the time]...yeah we don't never sit down...religiously and go through the whole round, no.*

Summary

When on the practice range, he and his player will often discuss the player's swing and he will help her with it. Come play days, his player is much more task focused and there is generally less casual conversation on the range. After rounds they will sometime discuss the round, focusing on the positive, whilst trying to improve on the negative.

170

The Player Goals and Game Plans

Q: Does [your player] ever set goals for a tournament?

A: *Not for a tournament, I don't think she does. I don't really sit down and discuss it with her, but at the start of last year I said to her…'what are your goals for the year?' She said 'well I don't really have any.' I said, 'well that's…y'know, pretty stupid I think.' I said, 'surely you should set some goals?' so she was like 'yeah, yeah I suppose I should.' I said…'well I think…your good goal for the year would be to finish top thirty on the money list and to win a tournament.' So 'yeah that sounds good' sort a thing so. Whether she…had that in her mind for the whole year or not I don't know, but I said that to her at the start of the year…and as it turned out she was top thirty…well like I said, I don't know if she really took…note of it. [It] might have gone in one ear and out the other. But…I did say that to her then…actually half-way through the year, I think it was; it must have been after the U.S. Open, when she did well at the U.S. Open…third…and that bumped her straight up the money list, and…then I said 'well y'know, you can re-adjust these goals now [to] inside the top ten on the money list.' So yeah, she…still sorta had it in the back of her mind, I think, but I don't know. Goals, you gotta set goals…she never had one previously.*

Q: Did she ever set them [goals] for a round?

A: *No not for a round. You can only play one shot at a time, so…I mean we [just] go out there…set the goal to shoot sixty-six; I mean you can do it but…I think it's bad actually, I mean…you can only take one shot at a time I suppose, so I think…a good goal's to…give a hundred percent to every shot; that'd be a better goal.*

Q: Do you think you will ask her [about her goals] again this year?

A: *Yeah, I was thinking about it the other day, actually, so [I'd suggest] for us to win a tournament, that would be a good goal….This year, I mean, that's what I said last year, but I remember saying top thirty on the money list and I don't know.*

Q: You don't think that was a good goal…for the year?

A: *I don't know; it is and it isn't; [it's] like setting money goals…it ain't quite right, I think; you should just set your goals for a tournament and slowly…the money comes…with it. I would say yeah, so it's not a here nor there type thing.*

Q: Do you or [your player] ever make a game plan together, prior to going out to play?

A: *Oh…game plan, as in like playing a hole, I suppose, like a tricky hole on a golf course and…*

Q: Only on tricky holes?

A: *Yeah, I mean, most holes are…'here's a driver,' you have to hit a driver…there's nothing but the driver. Some holes, it could be the four wood or the driver or something, so I guess that's about as much of a plan as we have….We've got [in] the back of our [minds]…there's…the conditions, whatever the conditions are well y'know, if they're not right or [on the] windy side.*

Q: How important is it for you to know about them [the goals]?

A: *Well…it's not really important is it? As long as she is setting goals…it's not. Y'know, if she's doing them, but if she's not doing it, it's not good.*

Q: You'd just like to know that's she's set some [goals]?

A: *Yeah.*

Q: Not necessarily what they were?

A: *Yeah exactly right….I don't care if I don't know a lot, but as long as she's doing it, yeah…whatever they maybe.*

Summary

This caddy has been instrumental in helping his player set goals for the year. However, he doesn't see this as a necessary part of his role (to know or be involved in the goal setting process). He thinks it is crucial for a player's success (i.e., for her to set goals), so he would be content in just knowing she set them, without needing to know the specifics. They also devise a rough game plan for more difficult holes. He believes that on a daily basis players ought not to set score-based goals, but goals that help them stay in the process.

Appendix B: EXERCISES

Exercise 1: GOAL SETTING

Date: _____

Write your dream goal here (How good do you hope to be?):

Write a short-term goal here (What do you want to achieve this week or round?):

What type of goal is this (tick one)?
             _____ mental (e.g., imagery)   _____ strategy (i.e., tactics)
             _____ physical (e.g., strength)   _____ technical (i.e., technique)

How does this goal fit into your long-term goals for the season/year?

How does this goal fit into your dream goals?

Is your goal **POST SMART** (tick those that apply)?

	Yes	No
PO - Is it a performance-oriented goal (e.g., % correct)?	_____	_____
ST - Is it a short-term goal (e.g., can achieve it today/week)?	_____	_____
S - Is it a specific goal (what *exactly* do you want)?	_____	_____
M - Is it a measurable goal (observable or statistical)?	_____	_____
A - Is it an achievable goal (can *you* achieve it)?	_____	_____
R - Is it a realistic goal (can you achieve it in *two weeks*)?	_____	_____
T - Is it a time-bound goal (do you have a target date)?	_____	_____

If you answered "no" to any of these, you should revise your goal.

What are your process goals or strategy to achieve this goal? Plan at least one activity that you have 100% control over that will lead you to your goal. Indicate the days of the week and times of the day you will do them (i.e., is it something you do in preparation for your round, or that you do during your round; if so, at what point?).

	Days (When?)	Times (What point?)
1)		
2)		
3)		

How much effort are you to give to achieve this goal (0-100%)?   _____ %

Exercise 2: SELF-TALK STATEMENTS

Date: _____

When reflecting on your day's performance, either as a caddy or player, sit down and complete this page. Record each negative thought you had and each statement that you said aloud either to yourself or to your player/caddy under the right-hand column. Then come up with a positive alternative that you could replace this with and record this in the opposite column next to the statement it goes with.

POSITIVE	NEGATIVE
• E.g., "Let's focus on getting it right now."	• E.g., "Don't stuff up this time."

Exercise 3: CONFIDENCE

Date: _____

Record all the reasons why you are a great caddy or golfer. Fill the whole page in making sure there is a different reason beside each bullet point. Keep this list somewhere you can remind yourself regularly.

WHY I AM A GREAT CADDY!

-
-
-
-
-
-
-
-
-
-
-
-
-
-
-
-
-
-
-
-
-
-
-
-
-
-
-
-

WHY I AM A GREAT GOLFER!

-
-
-
-
-
-
-
-
-
-
-
-
-
-
-
-
-
-
-
-
-
-
-
-

Exercise 4: MULTIPLE ROLES

Date: _____

Sit down with your player or caddy and complete this exercise together. Discuss each box one at a time. Remember you want to find a win-win solution (you are after all on the same team), so listen to each other. Repeat what you hear before responding to the suggestions of your player or caddy.

MULTIPLE ROLES AS CADDY

As a CADDY, my role is to:

I will be CADDY in these situations only:

As a PARENT/PARTNER/FRIEND, my role is to:

We would suggest that as a parent/partner/friend that your role is to provide unconditional love and support to your son/daughter or partner/friend regardless of playing well or poorly, winning or losing.

Remember that this is your DEFAULT role; in other words, if you were not his/her caddy, you would still be his/her parent/partner/friend. Therefore, when you are not being his/her caddy you are by default a parent/partner/friend. Your role as parent or partner or friend is infinitely more important to your partner or son/daughter or friend than your role as caddy and should be your priority role.

I will ensure that I am being a PARENT/PARTNER/FRIEND in these situations by doing the following:

PLAYER WITH MULTIPLE ROLE CADDY ROLES

As a PLAYER, my role is to:

I will be a PLAYER in these situations only (i.e., I will only talk about golf in these situations unless I ask permission to change roles out of the designated time with my caddy/parent/partner/friend):

As a SON/DAUGHTER, PARTNER, or FRIEND, my role is to:

We would suggest that your role means to love your parent/partner/friend unconditionally, regardless of how you think he/she ought to b e treating you or supporting you as a player.

Remember, this is your DEFAULT role, so whenever you are not a "player" you are by default his/her partner or son/daughter or friend. Therefore, we would argue that your role as partner/son/daughter/friend should take precedence over your role as player.

I will be a DAUGHTER/SON, PARTNER, or FRIEND in these situations: